When God Became ApParent

*The Early Death of a Parent and
The Lifelong Journey without
a Mother or Father*

Darren Daugherty

PRESS

Xulon Press
11350 Random Hills Road
Suite 800
Fairfax, VA 22030
(703) 279-6511
XulonPress.com

To order additional copies, call 1-866-909-BOOK (2665).

In Memory of

Daniel Daugherty,
the father I knew for thirteen years,

David O'Dell,
the father-in-law I will meet in heaven,

In Dedication to

Deborah Daugherty and Geraldine Casper,
the mother and mother-in-law
who have never seemed to mind when
the deceased were placed on a pedestal

Wendy,
the wife I cherish and with whom
I share everything—even the loss of a daddy

Daniela, David, and Jameson,
the children who call me, "Daddy"
and for whom I diligently build memories

Table of Contents

A Word from the Author

If I was asked to label one event in life as my defining moment, I could say that it was the death of my dad when I was thirteen years-old. I could also say that it was when I accepted Jesus Christ as my savior when I was five years-old; or when I further committed my life to Him at the ages of ten and thirteen. Each event marked a greater understanding and a necessary milestone in my relationship with God.

My defining moment included the death of my dad and the work of God in my life. In the absence of my father, my heavenly father became more apparent, and Jesus became a parent. I learned the truth of Psalm 68:5: God is the father of the fatherless. My loss and God's touch has been the primary focus of my testimony for many years. I have repeated it in preaching about loss, teaching children about God's comfort, and motivating parents to make the most of every moment with their children.

Combined with my testimony is my wife's early loss of her father—when she was twelve-years-old. Like me, her life has been impacted by her loss. She also discovered the comforting arms of Jesus and the truth of Psalm 68:5. Along with the words of forty other people, the impact of our loss is woven throughout this book.

This was a topic that I had planned to write about "someday," but I did not plan that my doctoral thesis would serve as the catalyst for this book. I had been thinking, "This has been a part of my life for many years. Do I really want to explore it further? What could I gain from this? Haven't I already figured out what this loss means?" I had already discovered the impact of the early death of my father and the ways that God had ministered to me, but I had not heard the stories of others who encountered a similar loss. What did this loss mean to them?

In reviewing the research on this topic, I discovered that most literature is bound to the effects that an early death of a parent has on children and teenagers. Most writings on this subject are also very impersonal—void of feelings and human understandings. A review of literature is located in Appendix 1.

My first purpose for this book is to help the reader understand what it is like to live with this lifelong loss, as described by adults. The words of others have created a richness that could not have come solely from me. Each reader will be enriched by these heart-felt descriptions. Details of the adults and data collection are found in Appendix 2.

My second purpose for this book is to offer insight to the surviving parent. Helping a child after this tragic event is not a simple task, especially when one is grieving the death of a spouse. I hope that surviving parents will be helped by the lessons that others have previously learned about this loss.

Although each person's encounter with the loss is unique, common understandings became apparent in our conversations. From these understandings came the chapter themes and sub-themes of this book. I have included my own experiences and insights in Chapter 1 and each chapter summary. I hope to help the reader to better understand this loss and the hope that is found in God when Jesus becomes apparent—and a parent.

Introduction

The main purpose of this book is to increase understanding of a lifelong loss that begins when a person experiences the death of a mother or father in childhood or adolescence. Each person's specific experience is unique, but essential aspects of the experience are common. This book is about what this loss means to those who live with it.

Key Understandings about Loss and Grief

Loss is defined as "the harm or privation resulting from loss or separation" To elaborate further, "privation" is defined as, "an act or instance of depriving; the state of being deprived."[1] Experiencing the early death of a parent is not just about an act or instance. As indicated, it is an ongoing state of being deprived of one's parent.

Loss and grief are not the same

Because this book is mostly about a loss, it is important, at the outset, to distinguish between grief and loss. Grief is "a whole-body response to loss."[2] It has also been defined as "The thoughts and feelings that are experienced within oneself upon the death of some-one loved. In other words, grief is the internal meaning given to the experience of bereavement"[3] Mourning is the expression of grief.

Grief literature widely addresses the fact that grief involves many different stages. Once thought of as a staircase, grief is most often described as a wheel containing different points or spokes which can be randomly visited and revisited—again and again. Bowman wrote, "Grief is one of our most common of life experiences...grief is a part of life...Grief also lingers. It hangs around like a homeless dog, an unanticipated guest or a guest you know is coming by but you know not when."[4] Grief may come and go, but the loss of a loved one is a constant reality.

Loss is an on-going absence

In the context of this book, loss is the on-going absence initiated by the death of a parent in childhood or adolescence, and grief is the deep distress felt by the existence of the loss. Most importantly, grief is a response to loss. Grief may subside, but many losses are permanent. When a parent dies, life goes on for the child, but something and someone is missed. Bowman wrote, "Sometimes an incident can remind you of something you have missed."[5] The birth of a child or the observed bond between an elderly mother and her daughter can be incidents which remind an adult that although grief subsides, his or her loss of a parent continues through life.

The early death of a parent may include a number of secondary losses

Mitchell and Anderson named six major types of losses: *material loss* is associated with physical objects or surroundings; *relationship loss* involves the absence of emotional connectedness to another human being; *role or functional loss* is experienced in the absence of a specific role or accustom place in a social network; *systemic loss* includes the effect brought on by changes in systems; *health losses* are those in which a person experiences the loss of a muscular or neurological function of the body; and *intrapsychic losses* involve the experience of losing an emotionally important image of oneself.[6]

In experiencing the death of a parent in childhood or adolescence, an individual may feel any number of the losses described by

Mitchell and Anderson. For example, *material loss* may be felt immediately and into the future as a parent's income is gone. A permanency exists in *relationship loss*, as the parent-child relationship has no possibility of future growth. *Role or functional loss* may be experienced as being a father's daughter is gone once he is deceased. *Systemic loss* may be felt as a two-parent family transforms to a single-parent family. Because a number of these losses, as they relate to the experience, are permanent in nature, the purpose of this book involves an examination of what it means to live, over time, with the loss and losses.

The early death of a parent is a loss of dreams

Intrapsychic loss, the most common loss evidenced in this book, was described by Ted Bowman as a loss of dreams. He wrote, "A loss of dreams, then, is a loss, as some writers put it, of assumptions. One writer calls it the loss of the assumptive world. Specific hopes for something that did not or cannot now occur, are dashed." [7] He further explained that the loss of dreams involves the loss of one's imagined picture of the way things were supposed to be. Bowman also pointed out that this type of loss is seldom addressed in grief literature.

In line with the descriptions of intrapsychic loss, a loss of assumptions, and a loss of dreams, a common understanding is described in "shattered dreams." Experiencing the early death of a parent involves loss in two major categories defined by Rando: physical (tangible) and psychosocial (intangible). [8] A person who experiences the death of a loved-one loses both. Rando described the loss of an intangible as having a dream shattered.

Usefulness of this Book

The understandings of the experience described in this book are important because they disclose what much of literature does not. As evidenced in Appendix 1, much of the existing literature involves the relation of variables in the lives of individuals who experienced the death of a parent. Such studies are valuable and necessary, but they do not usually include the personal understandings that individuals attach to their experience. Instead of a search to determine why or how individuals are affected by the death of a parent, this book is about understanding what it is like and what it means to live with the experience.

Other adults living with this loss

The meaning of the experience is useful in a number of different ways. First of all, adults who experienced the early death of a parent will find it useful to read about the experiences of others. This book may help them to better understand themselves and the ways in which they have related to their loss. These individuals may also come to recognize instances in which their loss has impacted other areas of life.

Surviving parents

Much of what is described in this book will help surviving parents to understand their children's view of the loss. As discussed throughout this book, the death of a parent in childhood or adolescence is not simply an event that one "gets over." It is an event that shapes the development of a person and continues throughout life, touching many different life experiences. At the end of chapters 2–9 is a section specifically written for surviving parents and other adults who are in contact with children or teenagers who have experienced the early death of a parent. These chapter endings consist of a list of suggestions based upon the descriptions of adults who experienced the early death of a parent.

Professionals

This book will also be useful to professionals who desire to gain a greater understanding of families and the issues that confront them. Such understandings may prove to be useful in helping family members touched by the early death of a parent. Clergy, counselors, and other professionals connected to issues of death and grief will find this book to be very useful to their own understanding and work. Ultimately, the purpose of this book is to increase understanding for every person who reads it, whether they be a professional, a participant, or a curious reader.

Persons touched by any loss

This book could not be written without the acknowledgement of God's grace, presence, comfort, guidance, and sacrifice. It is important for each person touched by such a loss to ask, "What does God want to do in and through me as a result of this loss?" Three facts remain clear as we trust in Jesus: He does not allow more hardship than we can bear; He will bring strength out of our tragedy; He will be with us through every moment of our loss. Christ not only helps us through the difficulties in life; He also uses them to make us into better people. If you have been touched by the early death of a parent, have faith in Jesus.

In the interviews for this book, conversations were not scripted, yet a number of individuals initiated conversation about the importance of their faith in relation to their loss. Not everyone spoke of a faith in Christ, and the number of Christians was not known. Regardless, persons described their loss with deep feelings that will help the reader to better understand this loss. For the author and many others, God became apparent amidst their loss, and He will do the same for anyone who seeks Him.

A Childhood Loss that Is Lifelong

What does it mean to live with the loss experienced through the early death of a parent? It is about more than the loss of a parent in childhood or adolescence; it is also about living with this loss in adulthood. Much has been researched, with the use of both quantitative and qualitative methodologies, about how parental loss affects children and adolescents. The individuals who contributed to this book were not asked to simply describe an event from their developmental years; they were asked to explain those meanings that they have attached to their loss.

It may be more or less common than you think

Data indicates that about 1.5 million youth—five percent of the population—experience the death of a parent by age fifteen.[9] Studies have also shown that parental loss in childhood and adolescence is an important topic for research. Wessel recognized this phenomenon in his pediatric practice:

As I inquired about details of a family's medical history, I discovered that many expectant parents had suffered the loss of a parent during childhood. I was surprised that many men and women cried as they shared memories of their losses during the first decade of their life.[10]

Heinzer wrote, "Parental death in childhood is considered a major loss, one that could have a serious impact on adaptation in adolescence and later adulthood."[11] Furman also emphasized the magnitude of this loss when she wrote,

Of all the losses through death, parental bereavement in childhood is unique in itself. It involves the loss of a love object whose emotional investment far exceeds any relationship in later life...In childhood, moreover, the parent is not only the major loved one, he or she is also a part of the child's self...[12]

It is an event that reverberates throughout life

The life-experience described in this book is a loss that began with one event—at a specific time. It continues as a way of life—throughout time. Along the journey, the ages of deceased parents do not change, and their children often hold inner representations of which are both frozen in time and timeless.[13] Such representations can be frozen for an entire lifetime. Mourners often keep memories alive by integrating them into the present and into relationships with others.[14] As Simon and Drantell wrote, "...losing a parent to death in childhood is a life event that keeps on reverberating long into adulthood."[15]

It is a loss to be understood

It is important for those who experienced the early death of a parent to make some sense of their loss—an endeavor in which this book can be a tool. Wright spoke to the importance of openly dealing with childhood losses, such as the death of a parent: "The losses of our adult life may be compounded by the remaining unresolved losses of our childhood. We bring these into our adult life like unwelcome excess baggage." [16] Like many authors on this subject, he also discussed the reality of life-long memories initiated by a childhood loss: "We all perceive life from our backlog of experiences because our memories are always with us. Our perceptions happen automatically, and we believe that what we perceive is actually the real world." [17]

As with most childhood events and changes, different understandings come with age. To this issue, Wright said,

Whenever a loss occurs, it is important to see it in the context of your life experiences so you understand the full impact of what has happened. Identifying all of the accompanying losses as well as the impact of this loss on your thinking toward future events is important. [18]

Hickman wrote of an optimistic future with loss, "...we can know that, down the road, our gratitude for the life of the person will far outstrip the terrible grief that at first seems to take up the whole landscape of our lives...it will take time before the scale, tipped initially with the primary weight of grief, rebalances itself..." [19]

It "never" happens, but it is permanent

Living with the loss of a parent in childhood or adolescence involves acknowledgement that certain expectations or assumptions about life are permanently gone. One woman said: "... people never divorced and parents didn't die. So, of course, this was a tremendous loss." Even in cases with terminally ill parents, it is not always expected that the parent will die. One man was seventeen when his mother died—an age at which he understood the fatal effect of cancer. He knew all about chemotherapy and the seriousness of the illness, yet he explained, "You think, 'She's sick and she'll get better.' One time she goes to the hospital and she doesn't come back." Those who experienced the early death of a parent received an early education in the permanence of death.

Earl Grollman wrote,

> Your loved one has died.
> You are unprepared.
> The death has struck you like a tidal wave.
> You are cut loose from your moorings.
> You are all but drowning in the sea of your private sorrow.
> The person who has been part of your life is gone forever.
> It is final, irrevocable.
> Part of you has died.[20]

Introduction to the Main Themes

The titles of chapters 2–9 represent the main themes that were discovered in examining the stories of adults who experienced the early death of a mother or father. The main themes are: *A Parent's Death as the Marker Between Two Lives; Living with Childhood Memories of Loss; Childhood Loss Now Seen through Adult Eyes; Constant Awareness of Mortality; Absence of the Parent throughout the Remainder of Life; Presence of the Parent in Memory throughout the Remainder of Life; Understanding and Defining Self; Influence of Loss in Family Living.*

Chapter 1

Daddy, We're Going Home Now

A Personal Story

The Waiting Room

We sat in the waiting room, down the hall from my dad's hospital room. Two rows of chairs faced each other. I sat on one side, and my mom sat on the other, next to relatives. My dad had been in the hospital before, but this time was different. There were more people this time. Most sat in silence.

I hadn't visited him every night in the hospital, and now I was wishing that I would have. I didn't sense an urgency. I believed that he would be home soon. That night, I was hit with the realization that my dad, at thirty-eight years of age, would probably die.

A few minutes earlier, I looked at my dad in his hospital bed; the tubes; the heavy breathing; the in-and-out of consciousness. I talked to him, repeating myself until I saw a response or heard a whisper. I was afraid that the end was near.

Tears welled up in my eyes and ran down my cheeks as I sat in the waiting room. I looked at the concern on the faces of my mother and other relatives. Was the end really approaching? "I'm only thirteen," I thought, "This doesn't happen."

As I sat in the waiting room, I thought about family. I was the only child in my family. I enjoyed the closeness of our small family: dad, mom, and me. I also knew what it was like to have a large family. All members of my mom's large family lived near each other. I loved having both families.

As I sat in the waiting room, I thought about the deaths that I had already experienced. It started with my mother's mother, four years previous; then it was my father's father, two years previous; and then my mother's father, ten months previous. With each death, especially my mother's parents, to whom I was very close, I grieved and matured. "After this much death," I thought, "Is it possible that my dad will be gone too?"

As I sat in the waiting room, I thought about my grandfather. He was my mother's father who had died ten months ago—the godly patriarch of the family. Living next door to him provided me with the opportunity to be very close. We called him "Grandpap." He and my grandmother came to the United States from Italy in the 1920s. Here they found a land of opportunity and a personal relationship with Jesus Christ.

I often sat and listened to Grandpap, either in his barbershop or on the brick wall next to his house. Every conversation included Jesus, and I don't remember Grandpap ever talking about the love of Jesus without crying. He had a passion for God, greater than anyone I have yet to meet, and he was determined to tell everyone about his Savior. Grandpap would witness to every person that sat in his barber chair and every person that he talked to on the street. His motto was, "A sermon and a haircut for fifty cents." He always posed the question, "How can I stand before God someday without having shared Him with everyone that I met?"

As I sat in the waiting room, I remembered one unpleasant conversation with Grandpap. It took place about three years previous. As he told me the importance of living for Jesus, he pointed out that my dad was living a life apart from God. I knew that Grandpap's observation was true, yet it hurt my feelings. My dad didn't come to church with us; he didn't seem interested in serving God. I also knew that my dad's spiritual condition had recently worsened. After being diagnosed with Lymphoma, he was using more foul language, becoming extremely bothered by little things, and losing his temper. Grandpap's conversation was prompted by the fact that my dad came home drunk the night before. I had never known my dad to be drunk and that upset, but I knew what prompted his recent inner turmoil.

As I sat in the waiting room, I thought about my father's spiritual journey. It began three years previous. He went to the hospital, after discovering large lumps on his waistline. Doctors were concerned that it might be cancer. Our neighbor had just lost a long battle with cancer, and the entire neighborhood saw the pain that he and his family went through. My dad became an angry person during those weeks of waiting.

The day came in which my dad had to go through extensive medical tests. I understood that he was concerned. I also heard the worry in my mom's voice and saw it on her face. I didn't know what to think. I prayed to the Jesus that I had come to know—the Jesus in which Grandpap put so much faith.

While my dad was in the hospital, going through testing, my mom came home to meet me after school. I was in the kitchen when I heard the phone ring. Within a few minutes my mom called me into her bedroom. I found her kneeling by the bed, with the phone in her hand and tears in her eyes. I kneeled down at the opposite side of the bed and asked, "What's wrong." She said, "Daddy just gave his heart to Jesus." I can't describe the flood of emotions that I felt. I can only say that I can feel them again as I put these words in print. I don't remember crying tears of joy before this event in my life, but they began to flow down my face. There had been a great gap in our family. My father and Heavenly Father were always so far apart. At that moment, the gap was filled.

My dad was a new man. No longer would my mother and I go to church without him—he led the way; no longer would he stop at the bar for a few hours on his way home from work—he was home with us; no longer did we just say, "Good night," when it was time for bed—he read the Bible and we prayed together. Until that time, all the Christians that I knew were people that had known Jesus for many years. In my dad, I saw the life-changing power of Jesus first-hand.

"Lymphoma," "radiation," and "chemotherapy" were words that I quickly became familiar with at the age of ten. My dad seemed very healthy on most days. He was a strong bricklayer that worked throughout the week and received medical treatment on the week-end. Many weekends were very tough for him, dealing with muscle cramps and vomiting, but the weekdays seemed to go reasonably well. He was still very active. When one of the parents in our neighborhood would come out and play ball with the kids in the neighborhood—it was my dad; when a parent would go sledding with the kids in the neighborhood—it was my dad. Besides activities like hunting and fishing, my dad simply enjoyed being active and being outside. Although weekends were physically tough for him, he usually didn't seem very sick to me. I had always expected the weekend sickness to subside in time, but it didn't.

As I sat in the waiting room, I thought about how God had been preparing me for what seemed inevitable. When I was thirteen years old, we went on a family vacation to Niagara Falls, Canada. I enjoyed every minute of the trip, but a strange thing happened to me when we returned home. I went through an emotional roller coaster, which lasted about two weeks. My mom would find me crying in my room; my school teacher would see me crying in the middle of the school day. I may have seemed like an emotionally- disturbed child, but the reality of the future was hitting me hard. If my dad wasn't healed, he would eventually die. I wanted to have many more family vacations like that one, but I was afraid that it was the last of its kind. God was preparing me for the events ahead.

Three years after his diagnosis, the same year as our Niagara Falls vacation, my dad had to go into the hospital again. His blood count was very low, and his doctor wanted to make sure that things could be kept physically under control. Before we left for the hospital, my dad sat quietly at the kitchen table, wearing a blue turtleneck shirt and eating vanilla pudding. I stood quietly behind him for a moment, wondering if this was his last time at home. God was preparing me again.

The Last "Good-bye"

It was now two weeks after Thanksgiving. I sat in that waiting room across from my mother and other relatives. There was such a heaviness over the room—over my mom—over me. It was very late, and we planned to go home. My mom and I went back into my dad's hospital room. I stood at the foot of his bed while my mom stood next to him. She said, "Danny, we're going home now." In a blank stare, he said nothing. I said, "Daddy, we're going home now." He turned his head toward my mother and whispered something back, but we didn't hear it. We stepped closer. In a faint whisper, he said it again, "I'm going home too." My mom and I looked at each other, with tears running down our cheeks and smiles forming on our faces. I was immediately gripped by sadness. It hit me like a truck, "He was going to die." The sadness was followed by joy. Joy in my heart, similar to the day when my mom said, "Daddy gave his life to Jesus." My mom and I both knew that he wasn't talking about the little brick house that they had built on Woodmont Street. My dad was speaking of his heavenly home that Jesus had been preparing for him for the past three years. My dad, with all the assurance that God had already given him, knew where he would be soon—looking into the eyes of Jesus. As we were leaving the room, I said, "Daddy, I love you," and he whispered back to me, "I love you." Those were the last words he spoke to me.

The First Moments of Change

Morning of Mourning

My mom and I did not say much to each other that evening. We knew that this night would be different than all other nights. I slept in my mom's room, near the phone, but it was not a good night for sleeping. The phone rang at 6:00 am. A nurse said that we should come to the hospital.

As we headed to the hospital, we drove by my school bus stop, where kids were waiting for the bus. It was raining—symbolic of the news that awaited us. I remember looking through the raindrops on the rear window of the car as I wondered if any of my classmates had felt pain like this before. I also thought about how this day was a normal day for them, but a life-changing day for me.

When we arrived at the door of my dad's hospital room, a nurse met us and informed us that he had died. She told us that the last thing he said was, "Thank you for everything. I'm going home." He made his faith known in the hospital, and at the end of his three-week stay, he informed her that he would be "checking out." He died about thirty minutes after speaking to the nurse.

Expectations and Insensitivity of Others

I found myself standing at the side of his bed, thinking about the fact that he had been living in heaven for an hour or more. As I stood there crying, the nurse kept telling me, "Just let it out." This was the saddest moment of my life, but the nurse was making me feel as if I wasn't sad enough.

The next week contained a roller coaster of emotions for me. Children and teenagers grieve much differently than most adults. There I was, a thirteen-year-old that just lost a parent—sometimes crying—sometimes acting like nothing was wrong. The pain of people's words added to my grief. A few cousins and I were making paper airplanes in another room at the funeral home. An adult relative came into the room and lectured us on how improper we were being. I thought, "It was *my* dad that died, and I need some relief." Once again, I felt like I wasn't being sad enough.

Two of my dad's relatives had stopped by the funeral home to pay their respects. My dad's family was not as close as my mom's, but I was glad that they came. After visiting for a few moments, they had to leave. The last thing that one of them said to my mom was, "I'll be over to pick up my fishing poles next week." We were both hurt by that statement. My dad was dead, and he was thinking about fishing poles. I wanted to return the fishing poles in pieces. My dad deserved more respect than that.

The next evening my mom and I experienced something that is simply hard to believe. We were at the funeral home during evening visitation. As I was talking to someone, I noticed, out of the corner of my eye, that my mom was getting upset. The woman that she was talking to was saying something hurtful. I made my way to my mom just as the lady was leaving. I said, "Mom, what's wrong? What did she say?" "She told me that Daddy was not healed because he must have had unconfessed sin in his life and we did not have enough faith," my mom replied. I felt like a knife went into my heart. I saw what my dad was before Jesus; I saw the dramatic change that took place in his life three years ago; I saw the assurance that he had on his deathbed. I stood there with my mom, who was grieving over the death of her husband and now dealing with extra pain inflicted by a hard-hearted person. My father and mother and I had experienced a lot of pain and joy over the past few years. Not once did I get angry at anyone because of the pain. I did not blame doctors, God, my dad, or anyone. So, why would someone say something so cruel, and treat us like an enemy at our most difficult moment? I have no answer.

Within a few days, I was back to school, catching up on work that I had missed. Most students didn't say much, and most teachers didn't know what had happened in my life. That was just fine, because I really didn't want to be treated differently. The comments of one student stuck with me. As we were leaving wood shop and joking around with each other, a student came over to me and said something with a very sarcastic tone. He said, "You haven't changed much." I responded, "What do you mean?" He said, "Never mind." Once again, I felt like I wasn't acting sad enough.

The Closeness of God

A Precious Death

The death of a loved one can be an excuse for a person to stop serving God, but it is meant to be an opportunity to draw closer to God. For me, it was the latter. I felt more sadness in the following weeks, as the realization of my dad's death hit me. People had let me down with their words, but I quickly learned that God knew exactly how I felt. I had been doing personal devotions, each night, since my dad went back into the hospital. He had set the pattern in my life with family devotions, so I continued on my own as it was hard for my mom and I to have family devotions without him.

On the night after his death, I had been asking God a lot of questions that began with "Why." Then He answered. The devotional booklet, for December 6th, was titled, "A Precious Death," [1] and the scripture was Psalm 116:15, "Precious in the sight of the Lord is the death of godly ones." It was God's Word to me through Dennis De Haan:

The details of a loved one's death may be associated with feelings we'd rather forget. Through the tempering effects of tears and time the Heavenly Father graciously heals those painful wounds. But He also gives us that final separation an eternal significance and makes it one of life's most cherished experiences. The Lord assures us that the Homecoming of one of His own is precious to Himself. And our love for Him should make it precious to us as well.[2]

It was so clear to me that God was speaking directly to me!

Past Thoughts of Suicide

Two years later, my mom and I were looking through my dad's things. When he became a Christian, he began to have personal devotions, and he often wrote down his thoughts in a notebook. I hadn't looked at that brown, spiral notebook in detail. He always kept it with his Bible, even when we went to church. I found it in a dresser drawer this time. As I began to read it, I was stunned.

I knew that my dad had a radical turn-around, but I did not know of this one important detail. My dad, before accepting Christ, had thought of suicide—during that angry time when he had to go through medical tests that would result in the inevitable diagnosis of Lymphoma. The notebook read, "As I laid here thinking about the possibility of cancer, I looked for a way to kill myself. I watched others suffer through it, and I won't let my family go through the same thing. As I laid here, thinking these thoughts, I felt a presence in the room—a warmth—a light. I heard someone telling me that it was time to make my life right with Jesus and that God would take care of me and my family." My dad continued to journal the events of that day, dotting the page with what was probably his tears. God did take care of things, and God does take care of things.

Preparing for Future Family

When I was in my teen years, I heard a pastor say, "Boys without fathers will not be able to be husbands or dads." I was bothered by that statement. I had already started dreaming about the day when I would have a wife and children of my own.

The Programs

As I grew up, I became a student of family life, learning from programs in which most teenagers had no interest. My loss of a complete family gave me a greater appreciation of family; therefore, I wanted to be prepared to be a husband and father.

When our church sponsored a film series by Dr. James Dobson, I bought a notebook, furiously took notes, and never missed a session. I ate it up. Also as a teenager, I listened to *Focus on the Family's* daily radio program—growing in my knowledge of Christian family life and thinking of the future. I cannot adequately describe the great value of these programs in my life. Through them, God provided necessary tools in perfect timing.

The People

In my endeavor to learn, grow, and prepare, I made a point to observe marriages and families. Later in life, I realized how beneficial it was for me to spend time with my pastor's family—the Ridings, and youth pastor's family—the Troglios, observing their marriages and parent-child relationships.

The reality of God's presence was shown to me in my junior high years by a teacher—a friend of the family and a godly man. I am convinced that it was Mr. Bertoluzzi's self-sacrifice that helped develop in me a hunger for God. He invited me to his church, which soon became my church too. He and his family brought me to every church event. Most of all, he would have devotions and pray with me every day before the school day started.

Christian Life Church became a place in which I felt loved as a welcomed member of God's family. Many of those who ministered to me had no idea that their "little" gestures were monumental to me in the absence of my dad. I was the youngest—and worst— guy on the church softball team, but they encouraged me to play; I was a quiet teenager who was always greeted with a handshake by beautiful people who displayed Jesus to me; I was the kid who often needed transportation to church and special events, but was never stranded. In their simple gestures, people said, "You are loved." The wonderful people of that church in Trafford, Pennsylvania, ministered to me and sent me out into ministry. Their ministry to me was another way that God became apparent and a parent.

Living the Dream

Thinking Back

When I talk with my mom about my dad, I have difficulty referring to him as "Dad." When he passed away, he was "Daddy," so it will always be the same. Many years have passed, and I remember those days as if they were yesterday. They are frozen in time. God has taken care of things, just as He said He would—just as He told my dad—just as He told me and my wife—just as He tells my children.

Sharing Loss

A number of years ago I met Wendy, my wonderful wife. She felt the same pain at twelve-years-old that I felt at thirteen. Wendy came home from camp to find her mother crying in the kitchen. Her mother told her that Wendy's dad had been killed in a car accident on his way to a church softball game. Similar to my life, she drew closer to God through the death of her dad. We have contemplated the fact that our dads met in heaven before we met. Wendy and I are sure that they hang out together, along with a miscarried grand-child, in the presence of God. Until we see them again, our lives are about deliberately passing on a godly heritage that will last for generations to come.

Passing on Heritage

As I put this story in print, the ring on my smallest finger often clicks against the keyboard. It is a reminder of legacy, heritage, and family. The day my son David was born, I came home to tell my three-year-old daughter that she had a baby brother. There is nothing like being a daughter's daddy, and I would have been thrilled with another girl, but Daniela prayed for a brother. She also told everyone at church that God was going to give her one. In the meantime, Wendy and I wondered if God told her something that He had not told us. We also wondered if we would soon be counseling our daughter through the disappointment of a baby sister.

As I was changing my clothes, my eyes focused on an opened jewelry box on my dresser. There sat the ring that my dad bought for me in Colorado, the same year he died. I had never worn it, mostly because it was too big for me as a child. By coincidence or providence, I saw the ring and decided that the day of my son's birth would be the perfect day to start wearing it. That ring has become the Daugherty-family ring, and each of us has one just like it. It serves as a reminder that our lives are not just about us, but those who have gone before and those who will follow.

I have the family that I used to dream of when I was a teenager. Except for God, there is nothing more important to me than this family. My wife and I have been blessed with three wonderful, biological children, and are seeking to adopt children who need a loving family. Wendy and I often think about how close our dads and children would be. We realize that there is a part of life that our children will not experience: getting to know their grandpas. We also know the unwavering love of God in our lives, and we thank Him that He ministers to our children too. Although they cannot talk to their grandpas, they can talk to Jesus—the One who made them with a purpose—the One who has had His hand on their family and individual lives. Although they may opt for a more "mature" title for me someday, for now they call me, "Daddy."

Making Memories

A few years ago, I viewed *My Life*, a 1993 movie staring Michael Keaton and Nicole Kidman.[3] It is about a family that experiences cancer. Michael Keaton's character is a successful businessman living in California with his wife. They are dealing with two very significant life events: his diagnosis with cancer and the anticipation of their first baby. At many different moments throughout the movie, Keaton's character is seen talking into the lens of a video camera, offering advice to the child who may never know him. He teaches his future child about shooting basketball, dating girls, and appreciating his or her mother.

At the end of the movie, the viewer sees Keaton's character reading Green Eggs and Ham to his child. It seems that he has beaten the cancer. As the camera backs up, it becomes apparent that the little boy is watching a video tape of his father. On top of the television are piles of home videos. The little boy say, "Da Da," to which his mother confirms, "Yeah, Da Da."

I have become a memory-maker for my children, because I know what it is like to want more memories, and I know that life is unpredictable. As exhibited by Michael Keaton's character, parents would spend more time investing in their children's future if they knew that their own lives would soon be ending. Most of us do not have such a luxury; therefore, I am determined to take advantage of every day—every opportunity. Hope Edelman described this attitude. She explained that in experiencing the death of her mother when she was seventeen, her attitude toward everyday life was affected:

> You can look at life and think, "My God. Every day that you have is so precious and so important." When somebody dies you realize that if they had to do it all over again they wouldn't want to win the Pulitzer Prize or make the best-seller list. If they had to do it all over again, they'd just want one more day at the beach, or to sit with

their kids quietly on a blanket somewhere and talk about something one more time. I think the experience of my mother's death made me treasure those little things in a way that I never would have before.[4]

Appreciating the Journey

My loss is like a two-sided coin to me. On one side is the existence of life-long loss and painful memories. This side includes the fact that my loss is also shared with my children. On the other side of the coin is an appreciation for life and family. It has motivated me to be very deliberate in my relationships, especially with my wife and children. In other ways that I may never understand, I believe that good has come out of a loss that could have been eternally devastating.

....

I will lift up my eyes to the mountains;
from where shall my help come?
My help comes from the LORD,
who made heaven and earth.
Psalms 121:1-2

Chapter 2

A Parent's Death as the Marker Between Two Lives

The loss of a parent in childhood or adolescence can be likened to losing a tour guide while on a journey through unfamiliar territory. In such a scenario, the tour guide knows the territory, the language, the delights, and the challenges involved. He or she is experienced in traveling various stages of the journey.

Suddenly, the tour guide is gone forever. With the tour guide's presence, the journey would have been traveled in a certain way. Without the tour guide, the journey will be different. As an inexperienced traveler, the tourist will be forced to determine the remainder of the journey without the benefit of the guide. The journey has been changed into two journeys separated by the tour guide's departure. Adults who experienced the death of a parent in childhood or adolescence are living out this scenario. Whether a surviving parent is part of this picture or not, the journey through life is changed forever.

The Difference

People come to understand and experience their lives in individual ways. When an important person is removed from a life, that life is changed from what was known. Especially if the important person was responsible for shaping and guiding the individual, the loss becomes the start of a totally different life.

Jamie, who lost her mother at age nine, described her loss in this way: "I identify myself so strongly with this life-altering event that took place in my life over thirty years ago. It is who I am. There is the life before the death of my mother. There is the life after the death of my mother." As illustrated in Jamie's words, this phenomenon involves two lives or two parts of life separated by a life-altering event.

Although the marker is not always so explicitly described, it is evident that those who experienced the early death of a parent often speak about what they once had and then no longer had. Olivia longed for what she had before the loss, and she recognized that life would not be the same:

> I felt cheated that I never got to say a final goodbye. In the past few years, I find that I miss him more today than I did when I was younger. I feel that I never really got to know him...I can still see his face and hear his voice just like it was yesterday. If I could just hug him and tell him I loved him. If I could hear him say that he loved me; to feel his strong arms from a gentle hug.... I would give my last breath to spend just one more day with my Dad—to tell him all my hopes and dreams—to laugh with him and feel his strong, tender arms hug me back—to be able to say goodbye and that I loved him—to hear him say he loved me.

Those who experience the death of a parent in childhood or adolescence are able to describe a life in which they felt complete, contrasted with a life in which they feel incomplete. Kim described a comfort and assurance which she knew in her "former life" but has not known since her mother's death: "I think what I have missed the most is that comfort of being known without saying anything. The assurance of love no matter what... It would just be nice to be valued the way my mother valued me." Quincey said, "Living without my mom is like being immortal, but starving to death. The pain never ends and it really never abates." She is alive after her mother's death, but part of her sustenance is gone. Although a loss may not be continually painful, there is a felt absence that began when the parent died and exists throughout the second life.

This marker between two lives brings monumental change, as evident in the words of these three women. Irene: "I know I'm a different person than I ever would have been if she hadn't died. That is the impact, plain and simple." Nancy: "I think it has probably shaped everything that there is about me." Brooke: "I believe I am a different person today than I would have been if my father had lived longer and been an influence in my life for more years!" They described a monumental event that changed their lives and themselves. The marker started a new shaping of life that continues throughout the rest of life.

The specific ways in which life was changed are sometimes too numerous to describe. Nevertheless, the marker and the two lives become apparent. As Zoe explained,

> It changed my life and my family life in so many ways that it's difficult to even know where to start. In a nutshell, my father's illness and death were the defining moments of my life and made me into the person I am today, for better or worse...When all is said and done, I do like the person I've become. I don't think I would be the same person if I hadn't experienced this life-altering event at such a young age.

Life was so greatly changed that Zoe felt she became a totally different person than she would have been without the loss. For others, the changes are not so numerous as much as they are vague. Vi recognized that her life without her father has been influenced by her life with her father, but the connections are difficult to explain:

> The feeling of him fades. The feelings of remembering him fades. Daydreaming of him, wishing, stuff like

that…That fades. Memories keep going, but they are the same memories. No new ones… You are growing up and you are who you are because of him, but you can't remember why.

Death brings change. When a parent dies in a child's growing-up years, the change is monumental. New understandings and expectations are formed as old ones are shattered by the death.

The End and Beginning

One who experiences the early death of a parent often senses that the loss signifies the end of childhood and the beginning of adulthood. Nancy's words illustrate the sense of being cheated out of childhood:

When kids have a longer time with a parent, they can feel more like a child. I've never been able to feel like a child. That is a piece of loss. Even as I was dating and marrying, that piece, I was always the strong one. Every now and then you want to feel like the child.

Jackie keenly described it as "immediate adulthood." She said that there have been times in adult life in which she has sensed that it would be nice to have "some" childhood—have someone else do the caretaking. Rhonda also explained that she felt a desire to regain a little piece of childhood: "I had to grow up faster and learn things a lot quicker, but I feel there was also a time when I wanted to regress. It was like—'just let me be a kid.'"

In very direct terms adults often speak of the death of a parent as the end of childhood. Alice said, "After his death, I felt like I became an adult." Brooke explained, "When he died, it robbed us of most of our childhood!" She also mentioned a loss of security: "I definitely grew up fast after my Father's death, and although I don't think that this was so terrible, it would have been nice to feel secure for a little longer." Kathy explained, "Probably the most significant part of this whole thing was that I was the oldest and only girl. I went from a regular fifteen-year-old to being the mother." Olivia said, "I had little time to grieve [my father's death] as my Mother became my 'child' and I became the adult."

With the death of a parent in childhood or adolescence, life as one knows it is changed forever. Secondary losses are also felt as new responsibilities are required. Does one really enter adulthood, or is one simply expected to assume responsibilities that are commonly assigned to adults?

The Identity

A momentous loss, such as the death of a parent in childhood or adolescence, usually becomes a prominent feature of one's life. This does not mean that an individual abandons all other identifying characteristics of their identity. It means that life was so significantly shaped by the loss that other forces often pale in comparison.

Blythe said, "This is what defines me, and separates me from everyone else...I am alone—grappling with my defining characteristics—trying to put them in their place and allow them to be a part of my past, rather than dramatically influence my future. But that is difficult." As Olivia explained, the loss is the marker between "who I was" and "who I am."

The loss of a parent in childhood shapes our lives with loss from the beginning of our lives. It is what we grow up knowing, and we don't know any other way—what it would be like to have both parents watch us reach our personal milestones. Later losses shape our lives in other ways. Sometimes I think they are harder in some ways. I seem to be less resilient as I age. On the other hand, my later losses don't define my identity as intrinsically as the early death of my father. I know who I was before my children, I know who I was before the death of my mother [who died in my adult life]—those are parts of my identity. I barely remember life before my father, so life without him is all I know.

Summary

What is it like to live with the loss experienced through parental death in childhood or adolescence? It means recognizing the death of a parent as the marker between two lives. For all, it is the beginning of a way of life that is drastically different from the former life. It becomes the line between what was and what is. It marks the point at which past life ended and present life began.

The life with the parent and the life without the parent are separated by the life-altering event of the parent's death. It marks monumental change. For some, the marker signals the end of childhood and the beginning of adulthood. An alternate shaping of life and self begins; an influence is lost; the creation of memories is halted. Living with the loss, from that point on, means living a new way of life.

Personal Reflection

When I experienced the death of my dad, it became the defining moment of my life story, but I did not recognize it in these terms until I heard it articulated by the individuals interviewed for this book. As a teen, I recognized that I had experienced a tragedy that most children and teens had not endured. At the same time, I learned great lessons about the nearness of God and the comforting presence of Jesus. As a young adult in college and my first church positions, my dad's death was the crux of my testimony. It was the first thing I would tell to new friends that wanted to know more about me; It was the most concise way to describe my life and my testimony of God's grace. I wanted people to know that I had been through one of life's worst tragedies, and I had found God to be faithful.

I am more than twenty years past the death of my dad, but the event continues to be the greatest defining moment of my life—it always will be. I talk about it much less than I once did. In fact, I did not mention it in the last two sermons which I preached on the subject of "loss." In the past, I wondered if I talked about it too much. Recently, I have recognized that many people in my life do not know this about me. When I answer a person who has asked, "What is your book about?" they often ask, "What made you choose that topic?"

Because my passion in ministry is focused on families and Christian parenting, people often assume that I must have been raised in an "ideal," Christian family. They are correct to assume that I have been affected by my family, but it may not fit their criteria of "ideal." I am grateful for my life and how God has used my loss to shape who I am and how I live. Through tragedy, God became apparent—and a parent.

For the Surviving Parent

- **After such a loss, children want to sense predictability in their lives.** The surviving parent should make as few major changes as possible. Certain changes and secondary losses are inevitable with a major loss, but the surviving parent should postpone changes as long as possible and instigate change only after communicating with their children.
- **Adults should not pretend that life will be the same.** Older children and teenagers especially need to know that you are going to be honest with them. Life will never be as it was before the death of their parent, because that parent will never return or be replaced.
- **Children should not be told that they will "get over it."** As seen in the descriptions of individuals interviewed for this book, the permanency of this loss is very real and lifelong. The surviving parent should help their children to adjust and prepare for living with this lifelong loss. The chapter summaries throughout this book include a variety of insights designed to help the surviving parent in this endeavor.

A father of the fatherless
and a judge for the widows,
is God in His holy habitation.
Psalms 68:5

Chapter 3

Living With Childhood Memories of Loss

Adults who experienced the early death of a mother or father are as tourists, left without a tour guide in a strange land. They have become experienced travelers over time. They have traveled a long way without the original tour guide, but the memories of the early stages of the journey remain fresh in their minds. These travelers remember what it was like to be an inexperienced tourist, left to learn much about the journey on their own. They remember the grief, which they experienced when they had to face the journey without the tour guide. They remember specific feelings of loss, such as abandonment and incompleteness, which accompanied their grief. They remember, with appreciation, those individuals who assisted them on their personal journeys. These individuals included personal trainers, direction providers, and those with simple gestures of kindness, likened to a cup of water on a long journey. Whether their gestures were a large or small sacrifice, they were nevertheless momentous to the tourist who was left without a tour guide. These tourists, now experienced travelers, also remember the ways in which they experienced changes in responsibilities within their own tour groups. Responsibilities changed when the tour guide was gone.

The death of a parent in childhood or adolescence is a life-changing event. The adjustment includes specific moments and gained understandings which are burned into memory. For some, the memories established in the first few years of loss remain the most prominent. For all, memories from the entire period of growing up without the parent linger throughout life. Living with the loss in adulthood means also knowing what it is like in childhood or adolescence. The death is a marker which precedes a life of uncommon adjustments.

As adults describe their memories from the early years of their loss, it is evident that this period involved the beginning of key understandings of their loss. It was then that the moment of loss occurred; it was then that life was changed forever; it was then that they began to ask questions about life and death, but not necessarily receiving answers. As Chad said, "...dealing with losing a parent when you're young is a hard reality."

The following sub-themes together exemplify living with memories of the early years of loss: memories of grief; specific feelings of loss; involvement of others; and change in family. Within each of these sub-themes, various examples are described.

Personal Grief

Grief is a response to loss. It involves internal emotions and external expressions. One's first encounter with any type of loss and grief is momentous, especially in childhood. For many adults who experienced the early death of a parent, the death of their mother or father was their first major loss. Whether it was the first loss or not, individuals forever remember the feelings that accompanied the early years of grief.

A range of realities are faced in the initial encounter with loss. One of those realities is grief and the specific feelings involved with it. The loss was life-defining, and the memories of grief usually remain vivid. Irene said, "I do remember screaming in the room as they turned all the machines off. I didn't think she knew I loved her. I was in a play that night, and I did it, reassured that at least this way Mom could watch." Another person remembered being surprised by his reaction to grief: "I remember sitting on the stairs that led down to the apartment and crying. I remember kind of wondering at the same time that I was crying, why tears wouldn't come." Kathy recalled that she immediately coped with the grief by pretending that her father was not dead: "When I got there, the doctor came out and said that my dad had died. I remember going into emotions—crying immediately. I pretended that he hadn't died and I pretended that he had gone to our cabin, and that was my mechanism for coping." With the magnitude of this loss being so great, people often describe being jarred and flooded with emotions.

Early grief can be remembered with great clarity and feeling, displaying that it is a revisited place in memory. When one thinks about what it is like to live with a loss, his or her first remembrance usually begins with the first moments of the loss. Sam, speaking thirty-six years after the loss, described his pain with great emotion, "…it was just incredibly painful… it was a physical pain. I guess that was what really surprised me the most—how much it hurt inside." Recalling the initial moments of living with the loss was clearly part of understanding the realities faced in childhood.

The initial grief felt when a parent dies is shocking. It becomes a strong memory as do the details which people remember about their location and surroundings when they are faced with a traumatic event. For example, many individuals are able to describe the moment at which they heard that John F. Kennedy was shot or the World Trade Center was attacked. Adults who experienced the death of a parent in childhood or adolescence also recall their initial grief with great clarity.

Learning about Grief

When one encounters loss and grief, especially in childhood or adolescence, he or she enters a learning process. In many cases, there is no one to teach a person about grief. Instead, he or she must discover grief alone.

Suppression and expression

How does one respond to the grief which accompanies the death of a parent? It is suppression, expression, or both. Mike, a man in his thirties, lost his mother when he was thirteen. He first suppressed the grief, but it later came forth like a flood:

> I don't think it really sunk in. I kept trying to wake up from the dream...the dream of her not being there. I kept thinking, "I'll wake up and she'll be here...it'll all be back to normal." I bottled up so much emotionally when my mom passed away... I was comforting my friends. I had a real close friend that stayed with me; hung out at my house a lot. He wept more at the funeral than I did. For awhile I wondered, "What is going on? Did I not love her?"... But the week after that I had a total collapse...I think it was emotional...I backed it up so much that I became physically sick. I thought I was gonna die the week after my mom passed away...pains all over—sick—throwing up...All that emotion came out...Maybe it was the realization that I wasn't gonna wake up from the dream.

Although Quinn said that he had no caring feelings when he watched his distant father die, grief became evident. He explained, "The thing that pushed the emotion button was at the funeral when [others] came up to me and said, "I know how you feel." That's when I came apart." Quinn also described another occasion, "A kid just looked at me and said, 'Your dad is dead.' And it was like then it hit home..." Whether it is because of societal expectations or juvenile avoidance, individuals may deny their loss or "bottle" the grief attached to it. As in Mike's case, the bottle may unexpectedly burst open. As Quinn described, someone else may do or say something to open the bottled grief.

For many children or adolescents who lose a parent, the loss is their first experience with grief. A result of the loss is an education about grief—whether suppressed or expressed. In suppression, a child or adolescent may be motivated to meet the expectations of others, to avoid the unknown, or to regain a sense of normalcy.

Ongoing and reoccurring

Grief can come and go in the life of an individual. For most, it is like a sea tide that delivers unexpected waves. Many adults have a keen awareness of grief's continuance in their growing-up years. Early in life, they learned that pain and grief come and go—often unexpectedly. One person said, "…It seemed that this loss was just so painful that I just didn't want to love anybody…" Rhonda said, "I remember a lot of times crying…I would journal during that time. There were feelings that came out in that journal that I never realized I had." She also recognized that growing up with the loss meant that times of grief would come and go. She said that it was like being on " a very emotional roller coaster ride." Mike remembered, "And there's plenty of times during the first few years in which you just have one of those days where at the end of the day you just cry." Another person said, "No one could understand how badly I hurt…Somehow they think people stop grieving after a year."

Cues and expectations

An aspect of learning about grief is recognizing when to grieve. Children, especially, look to others to show them when and how to grieve. Isabel's dying mother had been very open with her about the inevitable moment of death. She prepared her to peacefully accept that moment, but after the death, Isabel needed to look to others for cues in grieving:

> I actually woke up to find my mother dead…I wasn't really scared. She had kind of talked about it…I remember her telling me it was easy to tell when her heart stopped beating because I wouldn't hear that ticking anymore. I knew that she was dead, but she just looked so peaceful. I knew that she wasn't in anymore pain. Then my brother and my father brought me out of the room.

For the rest of that day, I stayed at my sister's house. I just stayed in bed. I didn't really know quite what I was supposed to do. I didn't have any signals... I kind of followed my sister's reactions to determine how I should react. At my mother's funeral then, I didn't really know *when* I was supposed to cry or *if* I was supposed to cry. I would just kind of watch my sister. If she started crying, then I knew it was okay if I started crying.

Like many children in times of loss, Isabel looked for signs that would show her when and how to grieve. Vi also remembered trying to make sense of her initial encounter with the loss: "My immediate feelings were shock. I smiled when I hugged my mom. I remember feeling guilty for that...I think the first week was the hardest week." Vi's words illustrate a lack of maturity or lack of experience with loss. In shock, she smiled, but then felt guilty for doing something which she believed to be inappropriate.

As previously described, children in grief often look to adults for cues of how and when to grieve, and they do not always find clear signals. The signals they decipher often discourage outward expression of grief. A number of people can remember the beginning of a pattern in childhood, as Kim described it, "of stuffing feelings." Children understand the cues which deny permission to talk about the loss or feelings of loss. Two men described the societal expectations placed upon them to "handle the situation like a man." Quinn said, "It's hard to explain the emotional things that you grow through. I believe now, looking back, that you just swallow those things." Zeke said, "I never cried. Boys are raised not to cry." They internalized the societal expectations and equated the avoidance of emotions with being men.

Many women can also describe messages which they received in the early years of loss. Zoe received this message from her friends:

My whole world had changed. However, I was supposed to pretend that everything was normal. Even though I had some very close friends, I felt so alone in my grief. No one knew what I was feeling. If I even mentioned it, a look of panic would come over my friends' faces. I learned to suppress my feelings and continued to do so for years.

Chris received this message from close relatives:

Anytime that Mom came up in conversation, I would get visibly upset, and the conversation would end. I could never tell anyone that I needed to hear about her...I needed to hear about this "wonderful person" who was no longer part of my life. The lesson that I got out of these repeated scenes was that I could not and should not talk about this— that I should just deal with my feelings on my own and should not have to bother anyone else with my problems.

Whether the others involved in the previous situations consciously communicated the message of "silence" is not the issue. On a deeper level, people did not give them permission to share or show their feelings. Therefore, a number of individuals remember being confused with grieving and figuring it out by themselves.

Adults who experience the death of a parent in childhood or adolescence live with childhood memories of how they grieved their parent's death. They remember the initial grief which was felt when the parent died, and they remember what they learned about: expressing and suppressing grief; living with ongoing and reoccurring grief; and receiving the cues and expectations of others who taught them to grieve in certain ways. These memories are recalled over many years. They signify the beginning of the lived experience; early understandings of the loss; the early shaping of personal identity.

Specific Feelings

Along with grief, which is a response to loss, an individual may experience the beginning of new specific feelings. Along with grieving, adults are able to describe specific feelings of loss—feelings attached to change—feelings attached to a void. The following paragraphs include the most prominent examples of such feelings.

Differentness

As a child or adolescent experiences a major loss, he or she often has a sense of being different. The feeling of differentness may be related to the facing of an uncommon loss or feeling underprivileged in comparison to others. Chris, a woman speaking thirty years after the death of her mother, recalled, "I have always felt different from other children who have had a 'normal' childhood—those who had a 'normal' family."

Children do not connect this feeling of differentness to living in a single-parent home, especially in modern society. They connect their feelings to missing a parent who was gone forever. This may be felt at specific times in which a parent was expected to be with their child. Billie said, "It just made me feel different than all the other kids I knew. At Mother-Daughter affairs, I had to take my sister. On Mother's Day I felt left out." Others spoke of similar events in their growing up years in which a parent was expected to be present. Cynthia described an incident in which she lied in order to "cover up" this detail of her life:

> I think I was embarrassed because everybody that I knew had their mother. This one girl said, "Well where's your parents? How come you only have your sister?" And I'm like, "Oh, my mother and dad live in Idaho." I created this big thing...She went home and told her mom. Her mom felt really bad, and she called my sister. She said, "Gee, we're really sorry about your mother." My sister said, "Oh well, we're doing the best we can." And my friend's mother said, "So how long is your mother going to be in the hospital?" My sister said, "What!" She was appalled. When I got home, I got chewed out. She said, "How could you lie, and tell people your mother was still alive?" And I was like, "I don't know!"

In some cases, the child or teen with the loss feels that talking about the loss could make another person feel awkward or create an awkward moment. Isabel explained, "For me, it almost felt like I was carrying a secret throughout my life, because I didn't really feel comfortable talking about it with people I didn't know. All they have to say is, 'Well, I'm sorry to hear that.' It's pretty awkward." Quincey described the same feelings, in connection with strangers and friends:

> People have a hard time relating to a person who lost a parent young. Fellow teenagers treated me like a morbid celebrity. People I had never met gave me hugs and gave their condolences. My closest friends, however, felt intimidated by the fact that life is so uncertain. It made them realize that their own parents were mere mortals. For awhile, they too treated me awkwardly.

The difference, as described by adults, exists between those children who experienced the death of a parent and those who did not. Persons in contact with the child who has lost a parent may or may not feel that the child is different, but the child does. The feeling of differentness may be a combination of personally feeling different and feeling that others see them as being different—having a different life. Perhaps those in contact with such a child feel a sense of differentness as they contemplate the fragility of life and the possibility of permanent change in their own family structure. Regardless of how others feel, the child who experiences this loss knows that his or her experience is different than the majority of the population. It is uncommon to meet another child or teenager who has experienced the death of a parent.

Incompleteness

When one loses a loved one, he or she may feel a loss of wholeness. Especially in the early death of a parent, one can feel that he or she is left incomplete. Brooke explained, "It is difficult to explain, but it's almost like a part of yourself is missing."

When reduced to a simple truth, parents are a part of their children, and children are a part of their parents. The need for a parent-child bond, in an emotional sense, is a deeper understanding for many. Without that bond or relationship, there is incompleteness—especially if the parent-child relationship was very cohesive. Chad explained the magnitude of the loss of his mother:

> She was always my main motivation to want to do good—to want to be good—to want to succeed—to care and try—just about everything. When she passed on, it was really hard. There were a couple of years after she died that I just felt like I was drifting through a sea of blackness.

Without his mother, Chad was without his motivator and guide. After her death, he was missing an important piece of his life.

The incompleteness can also be felt in times when a two-parent family is desired. Laura explained, "Through your teenage years, I think both parents give you balance...I always had that missing part of not having a dad." A missing part creates an incomplete picture, especially when the one holding the picture judges it against an ideal, whole picture. Mike felt this way about his family. He said, "After my mom passed away...that was like the end of family. That was the end of my family as I knew it... without her there...it wasn't home." Mike also explained that although a wonderful relationship blossomed between he and his father, the positive outcomes did not make his picture complete.

In summary, incompleteness is found in the premature ending of childhood and beginning of adulthood; it was in the recognizing that the family photo is changed forever. Incompleteness is felt in being without a parent that will never return; a parent with which most are not able to exchange departing gestures.

Abandonment

A parent's responsibility to be with his or her child throughout the child's life is a common, societal assumption. When a child loses a parent, he or she may feel abandoned and may express it with intense feeling. Rhonda described it in these words: "I was very bitter and very angry for her dying on me when I was so young—and that she couldn't be there for me when I had questions or wanted to share my joys..." Another woman, who lost her father when she was fourteen years old, explained her fear of abandonment in connection to her surviving parent. She said, "...it was awful, and way too much to process as a teenager... afraid everyday of losing my other parent..."

Children and teens may have a feeling of abandonment due to certain conditions. Laura spoke of her father's failure to make financial preparations before his death. "We felt like my dad deserted us...even though we had no control over it. I was a little angry at him because he left us in that situation. It's like that's song, 'You picked a fine time to leave us, Lucille.'" Quinn felt abandoned because his father left everyone with anger and no possibility of reconciliation. "There was anger. There was hurt and frustration. I thought, 'How dare you? You don't have the right to leave now. You have to face up to all these other things, and you robbed me of the chance of being a man...'"

The feeling of abandonment in childhood may also be described as a reason for personality traits, such as being shy, introverted, and guarded in relationships with others. About her loss, Brooke said, "It brought a lot of insecurity into my life at an age when I don't think I was really equipped to handle it. I always felt like people would eventually leave or abandon me...." Chris said that she had feelings of "distrust" in connection with feeling abandoned by her deceased parent. She explained, "I was always considered "shy." 'Distrustful' would probably be a better word for it. I never wanted to get too close to anyone. Why? They were just going to leave eventually." Another woman put yet another angle on the feeling of abandonment when she explained, "I find that one of the ways that this has affected me is that I'm always guarded. I can't totally open up. It left me with a lot of questions about trust, and the fear of being abandoned..."

What is it like to live with the death of a parent in childhood or adolescence? It means living with the permanent departure of a major figure in one's life; it means memories of intense, specific feelings of loss. As described within this section, one may feel a sense of differentness resulting from this life-altering event. On a deeper level, one may sense a void left by the death of a parent: incompleteness or abandonment.

General Acceptance

Simply accepting the loss as part of life was described as another way of making sense of the loss and recalling the hard realities faced in the early years. As previously alluded to, this acceptance may be related to an attempt to hide feelings. Olivia said, "I think because I was very young when I lost my Dad, I was more able to hide my feelings and to go on." This acceptance, according to Nancy, may also be linked to emotional immaturity. She said, "I think the number one thing is not being able to process it at that age." Nevertheless, a number of adults recognize that life just continued. One person said, "I didn't think too much about it. I mean, this was part of my life." Jackie explained, "We just didn't even talk about it. We just went on from day to day as if nothing had ever happened." Another woman said, "You do accept it as just part of life." Irwin explained that for him, moving on with life meant going back to routine: "You know, you get back to school and get into the routine of things."

Adults can also describe a conscious effort, in their early years, to accept the loss and move on in life. Oscar recalled, "...as I was growing up, I know I thought a lot about it, but...I just pushed it out of my mind because I couldn't do anything about it and just made myself move on." Vi explained it as another part of the process of making sense of her loss: "First, it was more questioning 'why?' Then later, as you get past all of that, you realize that it is a done fact, and there's nothing you can change. You just go on and keep trying to live the way you're supposed to." Another person's under-standing in this area exemplifies what happens in this process—one moves on with life and later comes back to make sense of it. At a later date, one can step back from the situation to understand it better. Isabel explained that she did this "...in order to really gain the perspective on the situation and realize...what you may have missed...Until then, things may seem just fine."

Caring People

Children or teens that lose a parent may or may not have other prominent individuals who make positive contributions to their lives. When a child experiences the death and ongoing absence of a parent, positive involvement from other trusted adults, whether sacrificial or easy, is appreciated. Children may not be visibly thankful or immediately grateful, but every effort to reach out to them will be meaningful—even though the sense of appreciation may be deferred until adulthood. Adults who experienced the early death of a parent have clear memories of those who were unhelpful or hurtful with their words and actions.

When these adults describe the importance of others, they often speak, with great fondness, of ways in which others responded to them in their personal loss. In a general sense, some felt that they received special treatment from adults. In specific ways, they received valuable, one-on-one mentoring.

Receiving Special Treatment

In an effort to show compassion to a child with a loss, adults often display special treatment. Their attention, which does not always include words, is given as if to say, "I'm sorry about your loss." Carl said:

> It affected me. There was kind of a cloud or haze or something there. We were always a little bit different—in a good way. It turned out in a very positive way, but perhaps in a bit of an artificial way. Had we grown up in a normal family where we had both parents, we wouldn't have been treated as nicely.

Because of this cloud or haze, people in his hometown treated him differently. He also said, "My recollection is that I used to get into trouble doing stupid things and writing notes in class and what not. That never happened again. Like in sixth grade, all the kids in class would get detention for something, except for my brother and me."

Feeling Understood and Valued

Most people have a natural desire to be understood and valued. This desire may increase in the heart of the individual who has lost a parent. At a time in their lives when they may wonder if anyone understands the magnitude of their loss, children and teenagers appreciate when someone simply understands that life has been affected forever. At the same time, feeling valued or validated is important to individuals, especially if they experienced the death of the only parent who communicated a sense of worth in their lives.

In contrast to other adults who noted special treatment, Jackie felt valued by her teachers because they did not treat her different. Rather, they treated her like other kids. As a number of adults indicated, they did not want their loss to cause them to be singled out from other children. Jackie said, "Even the teachers at school—I'm sure they knew what my situation was, but it was never discussed. I was just one of the kids... I kind of felt like everybody had been informed and knew not to make an issue out of it."

Quinn actively searched for someone to believe in him. He found this attention in a man from his church: "What I was looking for was someone just to believe in me—that was the basic thing—if someone would just believe in me. Then there was a man in the church... He just believed in me." As evidenced in Quinn's words, he sensed that this man valued him and cared about him. Dan also felt valued with an unconditional acceptance that he received from his grandparents and an uncle. In return, he wanted to please them: "There was an acceptance—an unconditional acceptance...I couldn't do enough to want to try and please them." A few adults admitted that they have continued to look for this type of relationship in their adult lives. Rita said, "Since I haven't had my mother to cheer me on, I have been looking for that in other people."

Having Someone Available

The availability of a supportive person is of great value to those who endure a loss. It is the presence—or available presence—of another human being. Children want to have someone *there*. Jackie explained that she actively brought other people into her life: "I think my strongest coping skill through the whole thing was bringing other people into my life that I needed, and being blessed with the people to be *there* when I needed them."

When at school, Isabel felt that the teachers were *there* for her. She understood that they could not change her circumstances, but they cared: "That first Mother's Day was very hard. My teachers were great. I mean, they all tried to take care of me and stuff like that, but it was still...They couldn't exactly ignore Mother's Day—everybody else had a mother." Nancy's account also involved school events. She expressed appreciation for the women that she "borrowed" for mother-daughter events and other adults who were part of her network of support. Sam's description included the presence of caring priests at his parochial high school. He said that they "were aware" and they "were there": "They were all aware that I'd lost my father... I always felt that they treated me nice...I think that they were *there* for me. ... I felt that there was someone *there* if I really wanted to talk ... I just never did." Sam's words illustrate the significance of a person's presence. Although he never talked to them about his loss, he took comfort in their availability.

Feeling Momentous Care in Little Gestures

What a caring person may see as minor efforts, the receiver may recognize as momentous acts of care. When a child or adolescent experiences the death of a parent, he or she has a heightened awareness of the attention and gestures which others offer. In some cases, it is as if the giver and receiver have a shared understanding of the gesture, which does not require words.

Adults are very descriptive in speaking about this aspect of their loss. Many hold deep feelings of appreciation. Amy's mother died when she was only two months old. On one occasion, Amy was able to visit her mother's sister. It created a memory that Amy vividly remembers in her seventies:

> My dad drove us out there one summer. I can remember her just being so kind to me and so loving. I will just never

forget the first night she tucked me into this wonderful bed
that had clean sheets and smelled so sweet. She called me
"honey girl." I just felt, "My, how good this is." I guess that
was a touch of what I was missing. I have never forgotten
that. It was such a neat experience. She was just all over me
with love when I was there, and that was so good.

Amy's words signify how meaningful small gestures can be in
the everyday life of one whom has lost a parent. Amy spoke of
another episode which the average person may view as mundane.
Nevertheless, it meant much to Amy: "There was a cousin of her's
in Des Moines. They had us over a lot, and the wife did special
things for me. She took some black heads out of my ear. That
sounds kind of silly, but that's something a mother would do."

Amy's descriptions were very poignant. First of all, she said that
a simple gesture can be a received as touch of what is missed. A
child or teen without a parent often appreciates any gesture that
gives them a small taste of what they do not have. Would a blind
person appreciate a short moment of sight? Would a person,
confined to a wheelchair, appreciate the opportunity to walk, even if
very brief? Would a child without a mother appreciate a brief touch
of being mothered? Amy also communicated this simple truth: In
momentous gestures, what is done is not always what is most
important. What is often most important is that the gesture is
"something a mother would do."

Oscar's story, similar to the previous accounts, involved one
gesture by an uncle. It was the only time in which anyone had made
such an effort in Oscar's life. He had no one to regularly watch his
basketball games.

I thought it was fantastic. I thought it was great. He saw me
play the game and recognized that it was his nephew out
there playing ball. I had something to play for, otherwise I
played for myself... The fact that there was a male figure
there who was interested enough to take *me* to a game...

One of the most touching stories came from Quinn. He asked his girlfriend's father for a simple gesture that brought him to tears: "I remember coming to him one night…I must have been fifteen or sixteen. I asked him to hold me, and when he held me I just broke into tears. It was…just the embrace. I just needed that." Quinn clearly missed the embraces of a father, and he was deeply touched by receiving a "glimpse" of the closeness absent from his life.

Appreciation for the little gestures is one way that adults recall the caring efforts of others in their childhood. These gestures taught them about the importance of people in the life of someone with a major loss. The stories are fascinating. Many of the small gestures continue to be vivid memories, illustrating their prominence in the memories of those living with the loss.

Recognizing Parental Figures

When the search began for adults to interview for this book, those who had a stepparent in their life were not going to be considered as possible participants. It then became obvious, through their personal descriptions, that gaining a stepparent does not erase the loss or the absence felt after the death of a parent. Distinctions were not been made between those individuals with a stepparent and those without a stepparent. Adults, who were interviewed for this book, were able to verbalize deep insights into living with the loss of a parent, whether they gained a loving stepparent or not.

Amidst descriptions of irreplaceable, deceased parents, adults also recognized that other parental figures greatly impacted their lives. Quinn actively looked for father figures. He found them in two different men. One of them was the pastor at a local church. Quinn expressed the importance of this man in his life:

> And how do you be a man? How does a man handle this? My pastor became my dad. He was more of a dad to me than my own dad… My dad was a *father*. My pastor was my *dad*… He let me talk. I called him pop. I said, "I have questions." He'd listen to me. He'd help me…

Adopted parental figures are quite varied among those who

experienced the early death of a parent. Many adults recognize more than one person as a father figure or mother figure. Many recognize extended family members as those adopted parental figures. One of Jackie's mother figures—the most prominent in her life—was an aunt who she lived with during her high-school years. She also looked to the mothers of her friends: "Some of my friends' moms...I've sent Mother's Day cards to them over the years... expressing my appreciation."

Recognizing parental figures, as described by those interviewed for this book, seems to illustrate the desire to be a son or daughter. The individual will always be the child of the deceased parent, but the everyday role of being a son or daughter no longer exists with that deceased parent. A parental figure not only fulfills a parental role, but enables a child to be a son or daughter.

What is it like to live with childhood memories of the loss of a parent? It means appreciating the positive involvement of others in one's life. As previously described, such positive involvement may consist of a simple, mundane gesture. Even those who feel a great lack of attention in the early years of loss may be able to recall the positive involvement of others. They may remember the smallest and biggest moments in which someone was a presence in their lives as their parent could not be present. They can also appreciate the involvement of others in receiving special treatment; feeling understood and valued; having someone available; and recognizing parental figures. Descriptions indicate the importance of positive reinforcement in the life of a child who has lost a parent.

Family Changes

Experiencing the death of a parent in childhood or adolescence means that much of life is different. Adults who live with this loss are able to recall, with great clarity, the ways in which their family was changed by this loss. The most prominent familial change was seen in the familial responsibilities. The following paragraphs include a variety of examples which adults shared in describing the change in familial responsibilities: the surviving parent accepted extra responsibilities; siblings accepted parental responsibilities; I accepted parental responsibilities. Adults also indicated that they shared the deceased parent's responsibilities among siblings, filling a parent's role together. Many adults experience one or more of these changes, but not all of them.

Surviving Parent Accepted Extra Responsibilities

One of the most obvious ways in which familial responsibilities change, following the death of a parent, is in the "double duty" of the surviving parent. In a number of cases, the surviving parent does his or her best to be both mother and father. About this change, Chuck said of his mother, "Obviously, it put more pressure on my mom to have to fulfill both roles. She did an outstanding job in being able to do that." Irwin also spoke with great appreciation for his mother and the way in which she accepted the responsibilities of her husband: "She's got to be a saint in heaven for the way she picked up the reins and everything and worked so hard." Within Quinn's description of his mother was great appreciation for her effort to become the provider for the family:

> And so my mother raised all five of us...She worked during the time in the sixties when it was looked down upon for women to raise kids by themselves, let alone work outside the family. She did all of it...I don't remember ever going hungry. She scrubbed floors. She raised doctor's kids. She cleaned their houses. She cleaned their apartments, their work places. And all the weight that was on her. I was thinking about my own little world imploding on me.

Quinn indicated that he did not appreciate all that his mother was doing at the time, but he came to appreciate it in his adult life. Kathy also said that she was not aware of much of her loss in adolescence because her mother took upon the responsibilities of Kathy's father: "As to what it is like to deal with the loss...I think that I wasn't really aware because my mother took over so much. She took over being both parents. There were things that my mom and dad would've done for me together, and my mom just took over the role."

Sibling Accepted Parental Responsibilities

A change in responsibilities, within a family touched by early parent death, is exemplified in a sibling's acceptance of parental responsibilities. This acceptance may be either constant or periodic. In periodic acceptance, the oldest sibling may accept parental responsibilities until he or she goes to college. A sibling may also move back into the home to care for siblings for a period of time. Amy's sister filled such a role in her life. She described the "motherly" responsibilities that her sister took upon herself:

> I do remember that we had moved to this area and I was in a different school in fifth grade. We were supposed to get up in front and do something, and the mothers were there. My sister did come. I was so glad that she was there, but I felt a little different. I think she was a little bit uncomfortable, too. One other incident that I remember now is that I never really had a birthday party until we moved into this new neighborhood. My sister gave one for me. I was ten. I can remember what a joy that was until one of the little girls said something about the fact that she didn't like green Jell-O. I was so hurt. That was so ridiculous now that I think about it, but I know my sister worked hard to get it together. That was just the mean kind of thing that kids would say. That was about the only birthday party I ever had.

The felt-absence of a mother may have been occasionally evaded by Amy, but one cannot help but notice that Amy missed many birthday parties. Since this was her only birthday party, this motherly gesture by her sister continues to be remembered sixty years after the party. Much like Amy's situation, Isabel's sister moved back into the home to fulfill a motherly role: "I have an older sister. She's about ten years older than me. She had to move back in. She had gone off and was living on her own, but she had to come back and help out my dad and myself. I really think my family's really close because of that."

Not all changes in familial responsibility are welcomed ones. Although Laura looked to her uncles as father figures, her brother also attempted to fill a fatherly role. She described it this way:

> My older brother tried to be that father and I resented it…because he would say, "She should be doing this. She should be doing that." I really wished I'd had a father so he could be a father to his own kids…I was very glad when he finally had a child and could do some fathering on his own child.

I Accepted Parental Responsibilities

Another way in which familial responsibilities may change or transfer is in the acceptance of parental responsibilities by an individual. This description of change is much like that described in the previous section. Both involve children who accepted parental responsibilities. Whereas the previous section included descriptions of one's sibling, this section includes personal descriptions of one's own acceptance of responsibilities that his or her parent would have held. A related theme—becoming a more responsible person as a result of the loss—will be explored in another chapter.

Nancy's sister accepted the motherly role for about five months, before going to college. The responsibility then went to Nancy:

> My mother died in March. My sister graduated from high school in June and went away to college in August. I became the chief cook and bottle washer. It was going from a typical childhood of being a kid. Before I was even a teenager, I had total responsibility of caring for a sister, who at that time was eight; being the woman of the house; and doing the cooking, cleaning, and meal preparation.

Kim also took upon aspects of her mother's role: "Probably

the most significant part of this whole thing was that I was the oldest and only girl. I went from a regular fifteen-year-old to being the mother..."

A few adults also described a familial role change in which they had to become a parental or spousal support to their surviving parent. Olivia said, "I had little time to grieve as my Mother became my child and I became the adult." Zac felt that he filled an emotional need for his mother after his father's death: "I remember when we sought counseling for awhile. I remember her making a statement that we were like a married couple. I was my mother's emotional support. I can still remember... waking up and hearing her crying."

Summary

What is it like to live with the loss of a parent that died in childhood or adolescence? It means that individuals live with childhood memories of their parent's death—memories of the early years of living with the loss. Understanding what it is like to live with the loss *now*, involves looking at what it was like *then*. Living with the loss started with the death of the parent, as did the descriptions given by those who contributed to this book.

If one simply explains what it is like to live with the loss as an adult, he or she will miss an important part of the story—the introduction. As writers or storytellers, those who experienced the early death of a parent begin by describing the foundational qualities of the main character—themselves—shaped by surroundings and circumstances. They are the main characters in their own stories, and they remember what it was like to be *there*.

The childhood memories are important because they are the beginning of the story, the beginning of a new life. They are reminders of how one began to live with a monumental loss. At times, a sense of pride may be attached to the memories of overcoming a tragedy in childhood. In remembering, adults are able to describe details of their grief, their feelings of loss, and the positive and negative involvement of others in their lives. They also recognize ways in which their family was changed forever, especially in familial responsibilities.

Personal Reflection

As I look back on my teenage years of growing up without a father, I am grateful for having Jesus as my early foundation; receiving God's grace in supernatural ways; and being loved by people who displayed Christ's love. How did I make it through difficult times? The grief and specific feelings of loss were real, but so was Jesus.

Since my mother and I grieved in very different ways, most of my grief was expressed to God when I was alone in my bedroom. I learned that grief comes and goes like unexpected waves of the sea, becoming less frequent as years pass. Most importantly, I learned that Christ did not promise a perfect life for me, but He was faithful to always be with me.

I recently observed a Bible quizzing competition that included two young boys who unexpectedly lost their father to a heart attack. I watched them, prayed for them, and remembered what it was like to be in their shoes. When I went to various events, in my teenage years, I felt what one person in this book called, "a cloud." It wasn't a cloud of sadness or depression. Rather, it was a feeling of being different—of sticking out as the one who experienced a tragic event. On one hand, I felt encouraged to prove that I could survive with God's help. On the other hand, I wondered, "Who in this room knows that I lost my dad? Do people know, but keep silent? Do people care?" There were times when I wanted people to acknowledge that they know and care, and there were times when I didn't want the attention. Those boys may have been preoccupied with quizzing during the time in which I observed them, but I couldn't help but think about how their lives had become very different than most others. I am sure that they thought about their father during the quiz match. They may have even remembered his voice in the recitation of the questions. No one in the room knew exactly when thoughts of their father entered their minds—no one except God. I pray that through their loss, Jesus will always be apparent—and a parent.

For the Surviving Parent

- **Children and their grief are often ignored.** In dealing with one's own grief, a surviving parent may overlook a child who seems to be doing fine. Like people in this study, a child may be ignoring his or her own feelings in a desire to protect the surviving parent from having to care for them in the parent's time of need.
- **Children need you to invite them to talk about their feelings.** They need to talk, one-on-one with their surviving parent, and they need to know their parent's feelings. Such sharing will demonstrate an openness that they need. The surviving parent should ensure them that he or she is offering an open-ended invitation.
- **Children need you to re-invite them to talk about their feelings.** As seen in the descriptions of a few people in this book, many people continue with their own lives and forget that a family continues to live with this loss forever. When the concern of others becomes less frequent, a child will need the surviving parent to re-invite them to talk.
- **Children should not be pressured to grieve in certain ways.** Statements such as, "Just let it out," may be interpreted as, "You are not crying like you should." Saying, "Cheer up," is taken to mean, "You are acting too sad about this," or "You should be over this by now." The surviving parent should not assume that children do not feel their loss when they are not acting sad. At times, children may escape the weight of their loss by playing at "inappropriate" moments. The surviving parent should also remember that children in the same family will probably not grieve in the same ways—at least not at the same time.
- **Children should not be pressured into "tell-all" sessions.** They need to know that their parent is available, anytime. When the surviving parent pressures them into talking, he or she is telling them to fit the parent's timetable instead of sharing when they are ready.
- **Children should not be given extra pressure.** Like most children with this loss, they have probably heard, "You're the woman/man of the house now." The surviving parent should allow them to live without such pressure. Saying things like that may

bring a quicker end to their sense of childhood.

- **Children should be told the truth.** Using euphemisms may confuse them and prevent them from understanding what they need to know. On the other hand, adults must be sensitive to the age of the child and his or her level of understanding.
- **Children should be taught how to handle hurtful words.** Protecting children from hurtful words may be a goal. Chances are, someone will say something hurtful at the worst time in a child's life. Many people have good intentions, but their insensitivity often makes matters worse. The surviving parent should become aware of verbal insensitivity that their children have heard, so that he or she can coach them through dealing with it.
- **Children will remember how others helped.** Whether it is an uncle or a family in your church, it will mean a lot to your children when someone reaches out to them. They may not display a visible attitude of thanks, but they will be grateful in the years to come. When people say, "Is there anything we can do?" the surviving parent can coach people in doing things for children that will be very meaningful (fishing, baseball game, doll show, etc.) People may also do things for children that will touch their hearts in ways that the surviving parent does not expect or understand.
- **Children need someone to pray with and for them.** They have learned that life is unpredictable and a large portion of their guidance is gone. Children will be strengthened through the prayers of people. Just knowing that people are regularly praying for them and not forgetting about their loss will help them to be strong and courageous. The surviving parent should regularly pray with and for the children, and he or she should also advocate for others' prayers for the children. "Is there anything I can do?" can be answered with, "Will you regularly pray for my children?"
- **Children need to know that they are still in a family.** When their family is permanently changed, children may feel that they no longer have a family. The surviving parent should deliberately talk about the continuance of family, assuring the child that family has been changed—not destroyed.
- **Children need to have family fun.** The surviving parent should make deliberate efforts to have fun, family times. Such times

do not have to be elaborate or expensive. A weekly game night or trip to the park will suffice.

• **Children need to sense love from the surviving parent.** Many adults who experienced the early death of a parent can describe the loss of two parents, because the presence of the surviving parent greatly diminished after the death. In losing a spouse, the surviving parent becomes solely responsible for the family, which adds greater busyness to life. As it is important for every parent to learn and speak their children's love language, as described by Gary Chapman[1], the surviving parent may have to be more deliberate in this responsibility—especially since the children have only one parent from which to receive love.

....

I will not leave you as orphans;
I will come to you.
John 14:18

Chapter 4

Childhood Loss Now Seen Through Adult Eyes

W hen the inexperienced tourist loses a tour guide in the early stages of this journey, neither time nor the journey is halted. Although the tourist lacks experience, he or she is forced to continue the journey. This requirement is the nature of the journey through a foreign land, and it is the nature of life. As discussed in the previous chapter, the tourist, who has become an experienced traveler, remembers how he or she felt in the early stages of the journey. The traveler also appreciates the fact that they made it through those difficult times.

As a new army recruit grows into a trained survivalist through time spent in training, the tourist on this journey grows as a person and a traveler. They begin to examine the journey, and its various stages, in different ways and with new understandings. They become more familiar with the terrain, the other people involved, and the process of traveling. No longer an inexperienced tourist, the individual becomes an experienced traveler. In the process of the journey, the foreign land became familiar land and the journey became an accepted way of life. Although not a way of life that they would have chosen, they have acknowledged it as their own journey—a journey that was thrust upon them.

In the early stages of the journey, the traveler may have been most concerned with continuing the journey. It is possible that the extent of their search for understanding involved asking, "Why did this happen?" As they grow, they may become more deliberate about understanding their own journey. The travelers become students of their own journeys, and they ask, "What does the loss mean for me?" or "How can I continue the journey?" They look at the scope of the journey and try to make sense of it. The answers to their questions may come gradually or in a defining moment or period, many years after the journey began. The understandings at which they arrive are often different from those understandings formed as an inexperienced tourist. Certain expectations were changed when the tour guide was gone, but new understandings were gained with maturity.

Living with this loss means seeing, with adult eyes, the impact of a loss which occurred in the growing-up years of life. For those who experience the early death of a parent, adult understandings involve translating the impact of a traumatic childhood event into the rest of life. Those interviewed for this book described how they lived, are living, and will live with this forever loss.

Defining Moments of Understanding Loss

Understanding the impact of this childhood loss is an on-going endeavor, although it may never be complete. This does not imply that understanding is a constant, active pursuit. On the contrary, many individuals understand their loss in defining moments, which are often a random occurrence. A defining moment or period of life punctuates the ongoing process of understanding the loss. Jim recognized a thirty-year span between the occurrence of the loss and when he was "hit" with it: "Life without a father never really hit me until I reached my forties."

In a defining moment of understanding, individuals are faced with the impact of the childhood loss on their adult lives. Jackie's moment was experienced in college, about seven years after her mother's death:

> I have no idea what triggered it. I remember being in my dorm room and realizing that I couldn't remember anything about the first week—from when my mom died until after the funeral....I had no memory of it at all. I ended up calling my sister and saying, "This is freaking me out. Tell me what happened."

Kathy felt the weight of the past, at least thirty years after the loss of her father. She gave this account:

> I cried, and I cried, and I cried, at a ladies retreat. I don't remember what it was that brought it out, but it was like God just let me know that He was my father and that He was filling me with a love of a father and a dad—what I missed. I can't remember really suffering with my loss until that retreat...I was definitely grieving the loss of my father—thirty years later.

Sometimes understanding is gained in a specific period of life. Rhonda began to face the loss of her mother at least sixteen years after her death:

> It wasn't until I was about thirty years old that they finally broke down—the walls I erected in my life—and I began to realize that I'd never really dealt with my mother's death... I remember when I first started hashing through things. I didn't want to be an adult. I just want to be a child... I just wanted to slide down the slide at the park...There are times when I still do...There's that little kid in me that just wants to come out when I don't want to deal with it anymore.

After experiencing the death of a parent in childhood, one may put off dealing with the meaning of the loss in his or her life. Whether due to an inability to process the loss at a young age or a form of denial, persons may not face their loss or begin understanding it's impact until years after the loss had first occurred. As Cynthia said, "People put it away for awhile and don't even think about it sometimes until later." Irwin admitted, "I just didn't realize, at the time, how things were going to be...It wasn't until the later years that I realized what I had missed."

Following the loss, life may continue without much contemplation. Then years into adulthood, one may begin to understand the loss in new and different ways. Understanding continues throughout life. Sam, a man in his forties, who experienced the death of his father when he was twelve, said, "It's only kind of recently that I can even think about it without it hurting." Still others admitted that they have just begun the journey of understanding the impact of their parent's death. Chris said, "I have to quit being the person everybody else wants me to be, and be the person I became in order to survive. I am just starting on this journey, and have a long way to go."

The loss of a parent in childhood or adolescence is a defining moment which may be followed by other defining moments. The loss defines a new way of life. The loss is often understood in times in which a person is faced with the meanings of his or her loss.

Different View of Loss in Adulthood

Much understanding of one's loss comes in adulthood. In adulthood, one has more life experience to draw from and a more mature understanding of life processes. As Zoe said, "As an adult, I am able to understand more of what the grieving process is all about from an adult perspective." In adulthood, people have perspectives which are different from those that they had in childhood or adolescence. They see through adult eyes.

Chuck shared a specific insight that he acquired in adulthood. It reflects a perspective that was not possible in his childhood:

> As my dad was being taken out of the house and on the way to the ambulance he was shaking my hand for what ended up being the last time. Several things I've thought about: Who endures the greater pain—the parent who

knows they are dying and is going to leave their kids or the kids whose parent is dying? I've done this see-saw of, "Who is enduring the greater loss?" I've always thought that it was me, somewhat feeling sorry for myself, in growing up without a dad...Now as an adult with kids, I've thought, "If my dad knew he was seeing the family for the last time." I can't even imagine what that was like.

At that moment in the conversation, Chuck became teary-eyed as he surmised the pain that his father probably endured. He understood that the loss of his father was also his father's loss of him. As an adult, with children of his own, Chuck is able to imagine himself in his father's situation. He can imagine what it would be like to see his children for the last time while being transported on a paramedic's gurney. In Chuck's childhood or adolescence, such a feeling was less likely to be understood.

Individuals, whether in adulthood or their growing-up years, may come to understand the ways in which the impact of their parent's death was also felt by others. Of her mother's pain, Irene said, "I didn't understand, then, the pain she went through." In reference to her father's loss of a wife and her aunt's loss of a sister, Cynthia said, "When you're in the middle of this you don't think that this woman's losing a sister or this man's losing a wife." Of his mother's loss of his father, Irwin recognized, "What must have gone through her mind at this time that I was completely oblivious of? I was living in my teenage world." In adulthood, individuals may be able to understand the pain of others impacted by the death of their parent.

New understandings are gained in adulthood. As Quinn said, "Adults can deal with it. We can rationalize it in our mind. We can think about it. We can work it through. Kids only know, 'Hey, they're gone.'" This does not take away from the fact that children also give meaning to their loss, as illustrated in the previous chapter. Seeing the loss is done in greater maturity and deliberacy as one grows older—constantly accompanied by the presence of the loss. Laura explained it this way:

Your life is busier when you're younger...and then you

realize how important those things and times were to you...You want to remember them. For a while, you don't want to remember them. They hurt....And it takes you a while to appreciate some aspects of the loss.

The early death of a parent is a loss that one continues to carry as he or she grows older. Seeing the loss through child or adolescent eyes is different from seeing it through adult eyes. Through adult eyes, one sees through a filter, which consists of more experience and wisdom. He or she is then able to gain new understandings of the loss and its personal meanings.

Balanced Perspective of Loss

As part of their exploration of their own loss, adults often make a conscious effort to keep a balanced perspective of their loss. In other words, their understandings of the loss include more than a view of what was lost, but also what was gained. For some, it is simply an effort to accept the fact that there may be aspects of the loss for which they will not be able to find meaning. As Zoe said, "I tell myself that there are some things in life for which we will never have an answer." For others, it is difficult to see any specific good that has come of the loss, yet they displayed a great satisfaction with their life. Vi said, "My life has been filled with so much good. I am very blessed. I would not trade what I have now to have my father back." It was very difficult to lose her father at the age of twelve, but Vi realized that life would be so different than what it is now. She would not want to go through the loss again, and she continues to miss the presence of her father, but she thoroughly enjoys her life.

The ways that adults try to keep a balanced perspective vary from person to person. For some, specific good from the loss in their lives is very evident. For others, trying to be balanced is seen in a simple trust that there is a divine plan or an unseen benefit that is currently beyond their understanding. The following points illustrate predominant ways that adults approached this part of their journey to make sense of the loss in their lives.

Receiving consolation in faith

On the topic of receiving consolation in their lives, adults express various ways in which their faith helped them to have a positive outlook on the loss. Receiving consolation in faith was not seen in every person interviewed for this book, but among those who did not indicate a faith in God, there often existed a reference to an understanding of a religious concept. Cynthia was such a participant. She expressed, "My reward is that some day, I will be together with my mom and dad. It's not that I do believe it. I have to believe it. It's my hope."

Among adults that expressed finding consolation in faith, a number of them felt assured that they will meet the deceased parent in the afterlife. Chuck, for example, said, "I feel that he is in heaven and someday I'll be able to see him and join him… Whatever image I'll actually see of him in heaven. That's a major consolation. It's an incredible consolation." Chad expressed the same view: "But, being Christians then, is a good thing because you can turn it in to a positive…I will get to see her. She's in heaven…And there's that hope for the future and hope of that whole reconciliation, which is a very healing thing." Laura said it this way: "I think by having a belief in an after-life, you always have that hope that this isn't the end…That you will see them again… We always have that hope of being reunited." She further explained,

> God makes the difference in how you handle a whole lot because you do have the hope, as I said before, of seeing that loved-one again. So it's not like it's totally over with that relationship. Though it will be a different relationship, and you can never recoup what you've lost, it will be a relationship that one day, I know that when it's my time, my mom and dad are going to be right there.

Laura finished these words with tears in her eyes and a faltering voice. This aspect of her faith was obviously very meaningful to her and very consoling. At the same time, she recognized that the relationship will never be recouped. Vi also spoke of her faith and the consolation of heaven. She poignantly expressed the fact that the reality of the loss is still felt with the consolation of heaven: "When someone dies, even though they are in heaven, you are still dealing with the loss. Your heart is still broken in half and it hurts. That doesn't just all of a sudden make it all better. It can help, but you are still dealing with major loss."

Faith in God also provides as a source of strength and comfort in living with the loss. Irwin said, "I tell you, one of the biggest things is my faith. People who don't have this, I don't understand, who do they go to?" Nancy also credited her faith when she said, "I think I gained a lot of strength through my sense of faith. It has always been an intrical piece of my life, and probably has given me the strength and comfort that I needed."

Individuals also express an aspect of their faith in which they accept divine control. As Belinda expressed, such an understanding does not mean that understanding is complete. She said, "It is still difficult to understand why the Lord took a mother away from small girls, but He is in control, and He caused good to come out of it." Laura explained that she has simply accepted the loss and does not feel the need to question:

> Most times, with pain you can have growth come out of it... Would I exchange it?... I would definitely want to go back and have a healthy father, and I would want a father for longer...but God has our lives ordered and so I guess I'm saying that I'm accepting, and I'm not questioning now...I questioned as a child...

Faith also means direction and protection for many. Quinn described a moment in his teen years: "I just looked up in the heavens and said, "God, you took my dad. So you're gonna have to be my dad. And so, ah, that's how I had a relationship with God." Sam acknowledged a change in how he looked at loss and life: "What I am now to what I was... And what I would have continued becoming. I don't know that I would have ever settled down..." Sam credited his faith as the catalyst that changed his view from, "live it up since you won't live long," to "make plans for the bigger picture."

Mike's loss, as he described it, was a way for God to give him specific direction in life that may not have been possible with his mother alive. He said,

> I loved my mom and I miss her, but I don't mourn it as much because I just look at it in the whole scheme of what God's doing in my life… it was like a catapult…it got me sailing to where I was…it may have been harder for God to work and make change…and maybe it would be harder in my life to make the changes, but I'd still rather have her.

As indicated, consolation in faith does not mean that one does not miss the deceased parent or desire to have them back.

Divine protection is also an acknowledged benefit of faith in God. Alice said, "I am thoroughly convinced, that because of my dad's death at an age when I was still a child, God placed a certain hedge of protection upon me. I have been spared much heartache that others seem to have." She acknowledged that life could have been much worse. Vi described the protection that she felt:

> I've heard that a lot of times daughters without a strong father figure can end up getting in trouble with guys because they are longing for that type of relationship– the physical hugs and all that stuff. I really feel that God protected me all through that stage because there were a lot of guys that I liked but they never liked me. And the guys that liked me, I never liked. So, basically, I didn't date anyone in high school. …And then that's basically how it went until college. Then the one that I liked, liked me…I felt God was just protecting me until the right one came along because he knew I would attach myself to that person.

Consolation through faith does not nullify loss. Loss is still loss, and loss is still felt. Consolation is found in knowing that God is in control and in receiving His strength, direction, and protection. How does one successfully live with a life-changing loss? Trust God.

Seeing the glass half full

Individuals who live with a major loss often try to have a balanced perspective by seeking optimism, "looking on the bright side," and "seeing the glass half full." This was illustrated by Nancy:

> I think that I have probably developed tremendously because of that loss, in ways that I probably will never know ...I'd probably be living in a town of eighteen—hundred people. I may or may not have gone off to college. I may have never taken the career path that I did and be able to move to the levels that I have.. It put me into a whole new situation. Because of my experience, some of those things I've taught my daughter are deliberate. But, they have also been tremendously beneficial to me. You gain many wonderful things out of loss. Whether it is the loss of a job, or the loss of a relationship. There's half empty and half full. I guess I look at it half full.

As also illustrated in her words, Nancy's gains from her loss are passed on to her daughter as deliberate lessons; therefore, her daughter also gains.

Adults also expressed an effort to view what they have, instead of what they do not have. Vi said, "You really just try not to think about what you don't have." Laura expressed a similar understanding—appreciating the time she had with her father instead of the time that she missed:

> I guess you have to move on or else your own life gets stagnated and you don't go any where you know.. So, when I look now, I look back with appreciation and thankfulness for everything that I did experience and the time I did have with my dad and...not look back with regret of everything I didn't have with him...

Years after the early death of a parent, adults may be able to perceive that life could have been much worse. Although their situations are considered "less than ideal" to others, they may find consolation in the fact that life with the loss could not have been as manageable as it was. Oscar explained,

> As the years went by...When I would sit down and find time to think about it...It could have been worse, too. I could've grown up in a family where my father was an alcoholic. He could've lived until I was in college. He could have been a drunk. He could have been a wife-beater. He could have been a lot of things—a lot of things I could have possibly learned from him and carried over into my own life.

Sam expressed similar thoughts about his loss and the nature of his father's death, which was due to a sudden heart attack:

> I wish it had never happened, obviously. Then I think about how, just so many other people have so many worse stories. I'm thankful for how I lost my dad... I think, there's always something worse. Somebody's got a worse story... It doesn't seem quite as bad when I put in perspective of so many losses...

Adults may also look on the "bright side" by recognizing how bad their lives could have become. Such was the case with Alice: "To look back on it now, it's a miracle my life didn't get really messed up because I could have done anything I wanted."

Recognizing other gains

Adults also hold a balanced perspective by recognizing other specific gains, not described in previous sections. Nancy said,

> I had some really great opportunities in high school that I was able to take advantage of...because I learned to

juggle early in life. Women do that. I think that part of it is learning those skills early—the independence. I learned what it was like to finance a household...I think I tried things more readily—that were more risky than my peers. Not a lot of people left my hometown, but I did. Those are some of the benefits.

Oscar described an understanding that he gained—an understanding that his own children may not understand. In speaking about his attendance at their extracurricular activities, he said,

They don't know how important it was for me to do that first of all. They don't know how important it is to have your dad do that. Maybe they'll realize that when they have kids and grow up. It's hard to say. A lot of people don't realize a lot of things unless they've had a loss and can learn from it.

What does it mean for an adult to live with the death of a parent experienced in childhood or adolescence? It means that in the process of making sense of the loss, one looks for insights that may help create a balanced perspective. Even when it seems that the negative aspects of the loss are overwhelming, people desire to find some benefit and value in their loss. For many individuals, the benefits of the loss are not seen until it has been lived with for a few years and into adulthood.

Specific Aspects of Living with Loss

Adults living with the childhood loss of a parent continue to feel the impact of that loss in their adult years. As one participant said, "it reverberates" through life. There exists a sense that the loss is still felt at specific moments such as with certain family members, in certain locations, or at unexpected times. Chad said, "You definitely will be watching a show on television and you find yourself getting all teary eyed." He said that this is especially true of him if a family experiences loss in their portrayal in a television show.

Behind his adult eyes are years of wisdom and understanding, which assist him in recognizing the many unseen aspects of his loss and how he feels it in living.

Persons with this loss can be faced with their loss in specific encounters with family members. Dan described this feeling when being with his in-laws: "You're part of it, but it's not family. It's my wife's family. I realize I'm part of that family, but it's not my family. I don't have that with a mom and dad." Mike expressed a similar scenario: "It's strange…I don't know if there's any rhyme or reason to it…Once in a while it just hits me when with my in-laws…I think to myself, 'I really wish that these were my parents that I was getting to share this time with.' " Mike seemed somewhat embarrassed by feeling that way, but he and Dan have obviously felt that seeing their "in-tact," in-law families can remind them of their own loss.

Conflict with one's own child is also a time when the loss of a parent can be felt. Irwin shared this scenario:

> One of the times that it hit me the most was when my son was fourteen. He was having some trouble in school…He had been so angry and upset with me about something. He came up to me, and right to my face he said, "I hate you Dad. I wish you were dead." I told him at the time, "Jim, you don't know how lucky you are to have a dad." I said, "I was your age when I lost my dad." It really cut me, and it hurt very, very much at the time.

Within his description is Irwin's recognition that his son did not understand what he was really saying. This was combined with Irwin's pain of knowing what it really meant. Quinn described a similar scenario: "I remember a time with my own son when he was young…He'd done something wrong, and I got onto him and I put him in his room. He said…'I wish you were dead,' so I let him go, and I left him in his room…That hurt deep." Quinn later went back to his son and helped him understand what his statement really meant to Quinn. Irwin and Quinn could look back on a journey that they would not wish upon anyone, especially their sons. They could see what living with the loss has meant, but their sons could not.

Finally, persons with this life experience may feel a sense of loss at random. Ian feels his loss every few years, but does not know why: "The loss does tend to hit me again every few years. I've never noticed any specific patterns or triggers." Olivia said, "It's funny how, just out of the blue, those feelings just pop up and hit you in the face. You never know when it will."

Summary

What does it mean for an adult to live with the childhood death of a parent? As discussed in a previous chapter, this loss is about understanding two different lives—two lives and the traumatic loss that separates them. The process involves understanding how the loss affects the "second life."

An aspect of this lived experience is a growth in understanding. No longer is the loss viewed through the eyes of a child or adolescent. Different understandings of the loss are reached when one can see the loss through adult eyes—through eyes with years of experience—through eyes with greater maturity—through eyes with greater wisdom.

Seeing the loss through adult eyes means that one has defining moments of understanding the effects of the loss. Those defining moments may be specific times or periods in life. They may also occur throughout life. Seeing the loss through adult eyes also means looking at one's loss differently in adulthood and feeling the loss in specific moments in adulthood.

Personal Insights

As testimonies of God's grace, Wendy and I have been aware of how our loss has impacted our lives. A number of individuals understand their own losses in specific stages or defining moments, but our personal understandings have grown over time. We also acknowledge that we may have qualities that are unrecognized results of our loss.

When I reflect upon my teenage years, sometimes it seems as if I am reviewing someone else's life story. My life is forever touched by my loss, but God has brought about so much good. I have moments when it "hits me," such as when I wrote the first chapter of this book, but the occurrences of such moments in adulthood are separated by years.

As for having a different view of our loss in adulthood, Wendy and I are more grateful for what God has done in our lives through our loss. Am I thankful that my dad died? I cannot answer, "Yes," but I know that as years have passed, the goodness of God has outweighed the tragedy of death. We trust that God is accomplishing His will in our lives.

For the Surviving Parent

• **Children will benefit, in adulthood, from a godly foundation in the early years.** Although their view of the loss, and its impact on their lives, will grow with maturity and adulthood, children can receive a foundation on which to build their understandings. There is no substitute for the Christian influences in the life of a child who learns that there is a "bigger picture."

• **Children need to know Jesus.** Faith in Jesus and His unique and special plan for each life will help children keep their loss in perspective. The "bright side" of loss, for the Christian, is that God will do great things out of tough things. Many results may never be obvious, but the Christian can be "...confident of this very thing, that He who began a good work in you will perfect it until the day of Christ Jesus" (Phillipians 1:6). The surviving parent should deliberately model and speak about his or her faith in God's sovereignty.

....

For you have not received a spirit of slavery
leading to fear again, but you have received
a spirit of adoption as sons by which we cry out,
"Abba! Father!"
Romans 8:15

Chapter 5

Constant Awareness of Mortality

A future of great unpredictability awaits the tourists who experience the loss of a tour guide in the early stages of a long and arduous journey. Having experienced one of the worst tragedies of the journey, the tourists received an early introduction to the imminence of loss. The tourists are constantly aware of "goneness." They know that one can be gone at anytime; they think about being gone at the same age as their tour guide at his or her departure; they have fears and hopes for the journey that were shaped by their awareness of goneness; they travel more deliberately, knowing that the journey can end at anytime.

After the parent died, mortality became a constant companion for the remainder of the journey. As a constant awareness, mortality does not become a morbid obsession or defeatist attitude. Mortality is a fact of life that becomes more "real" in the life of those persons who experienced the death of a significant person in their lives. Those who lost a parent in childhood or adolescence, learned early in life that mortality is a possibility for everyone and anyone; this includes their surviving parent, themselves, and others involved in their lives.

Knowing that Death Can Happen at Any Time

Living with the loss means that a person always has a sense that death can happen at any time. As Sam said, "I always had death on my mind...that it could happen to me at any time." Chuck said, "The mortality thing is sort of the biggest thing that has influenced my life. I know I can be gone tomorrow." He also said that it is what drives him to focus on family togetherness, be a good parent, and create many memories with his children. Mike said, "It just makes you realize all the more how short life is." He also said that his reflections often involve thoughts of his son facing the same loss which he experienced as a child: "I never take a trip without thinking about it." When Nancy was asked to clarify if she was talking about the shortness of life, she said, "Life is unpredictable—not necessarily short—but unpredictable."

Awareness of the possibility of death is heightened by the experience of the death of a loved one. Especially at a young age, the death of a parent can shatter expectations and assumptions about the world. Cynthia said, "I think the average person doesn't sit around and give too much time to how they're going to die; when they're going to die; what they're going to die of. They just think, 'I'll die some day.'" Most adults are acutely aware that this is no longer true for them. Jackie explained that she came to a new way of evaluating adversity:

> I truly believed at that time, that if it wasn't something that could kill you, it wasn't bad. I would think, "I can live through this, so it's no big deal." That was truly the way I gauged whether things were good or bad. "Well, that didn't kill me, so I'm fine. I can go on with my day-to-day life because this is not going to kill me." The only goal is to survive...If you stay alive, you're winning.

Jackie's description indicates that although a survivor may be living care-free or carelessly, the possibility of death is a constant awareness.

With death as an unexpected guest who may arrive at any time, persons may find themselves living in very specific ways. An

awareness of imminent death may also translate into an appreciation for living. As Chuck explained, "The value of living and what's
important—it's just the whole mortality thing. It's just being aware
that it could end very quickly." Rhonda said, "You really value life.
I think you understand more…We take so much for granted, and
then when you come that close to death, you really realize how
precious, and how few moments you have." Alice said, "I live more
seriously than the average person—wanting to make the most of
situations—never knowing if it will be the last…"

An awareness of possible death often means that one has a reason
to appreciate life and make the most out of it. A parent's early death
teaches one that life is fragile and should be lived with care.
Attention is given to living, since dying is a felt reality.

Approaching Parent's Age of Death

The age at which a parent dies is a fact that a child does not
forget, especially when the death occurs at an age younger than the
average population. The early death of a parent is usually
surrounded by the comments of others that point out how young the
parent was. The child of the deceased parent learns that numbers
such as thirty-three, thirty-eight, and forty-two mark the early,
uncommon death of an adult. Yet, this age, which is much greater
than the child's own age, is not reached for some time.

The probability of dying at the same age of one's parent is quite
low, but one who experiences the death of a parent in childhood or
adolescence, has a constant awareness of the age of his or her
parent at the time of death. For some, an expectation of early death
is attached to approaching their parent's age. For others, approaching their parent's age is a nostalgic milestone.

Individuals living with this loss may simply remain aware of
approaching the age of their deceased parent without necessarily
worrying about it. Zac said this about his father's age of death, "I
haven't hit that point yet, but I've always remembered it, and wait for
it." Vi exhibited the same attention when she said, "I'm not supersti-
tious or anything like that, but I think of it sometimes. I know that I'm
the same age that he was when he died. I think about how young he

was. I don't assume that it will happen now just because I'm that age, but it is in the back of my mind." Sam recognized that he is a few years away from his father's age of death: "I'm fifty years old and I'm hoping I live to be maybe seventy-five or eighty. My dad died when he was fifty-four. I'm getting right at the age." He also mentioned that his youngest son will be the same age that Sam was when his father died.

Whereas it is a nostalgic observation for most people, adults also have specific thoughts of dying at the same age as their parent. Chris said that she didn't look past the possibility of living a long life until she passed her mother's age of death:

> One of the things that I have had to cope with was the thought that I was going to die before the age of thirty-two, which is how old my mother was when she died. I never believed that I had any reason to make any long term plans or goals. Why bother? I am not going to be around anyway. Well, here I am. I am thirty-five... When I passed the age of thirty-two, it finally sunk in that I am not my mother. My fate is not my mother's fate. I will die, and that's okay. I no longer have to worry about it or let it control me.

Oscar shared a similar scenario that was on his mind since his teenage years and until he turned forty-six years old:

> For many years...all through high school, all through college, even in my early adult years...My dad died at forty-six and I had this thing in me that said, "You're probably going to die at forty-six too." When I reached my forty-sixth birthday and I was still alive, I thought, "I beat him." And then at my forty-seventh, I thought, "I beat him by a year."

Cynthia said that she recently decided to take better care of herself because she would like to live past her mother's age: "I'm trying not to be as reckless with my health...I have been trying to take care of me. I want to live longer, which is my ultimate goal. I really don't want to die at fifty." In her description was an underlying desire to avoid dying at the same age as her mother.

Shaping of Fears and Hopes for the Future

As one matures in life, the early awareness of mortality continues, and it often shapes fears and hopes for the future. An awareness of mortality is a focus that involves more than simply thinking about it; it becomes a focus with outgrowths applicable to living in the future.

Fears for the Future

This example is similar to the previous section, which includes the theme of approaching the parent's age of death. It is different in that the parent's death shaped a general expectation of a short life, which in turn shapes other aspects of life. Cynthia explained how it affected her when she first met her fiancé. She would tell him, "Well, I'm probably going to be dead, so let's not make too many plans." Sam related his care-free attitude of the past to his assumption of a short life: "In my early twenties...I was thinking so much about death. I just really wanted to have a good time—just in case I wasn't going to be around later." He indicated that he has regretted that attitude, because it inhibited him from pursuing a specific career direction: "I was never really goal orientated because I was never really sure how long I was going to be around. I could have done a little more with my life if I would have snapped to it a little quicker..."

Fearing the loss of future can be so significant that a person seems to expect to have no future. The descriptions of Cynthia and Sam indicate that expecting no future may simply be a defense mechanism in which people prepare themselves for the possibility of death. Their words seem to communicate, "Since death is possible, I'll just expect it. Then I will not be surprised."

An individual with this loss may also develop a general concern of early death that is not specific to the deceased parent's age of death. It is not necessarily a fear of dying as much as it is the fear of creating loss in the life of someone else. Most adults in this study have children, which contributes to their concern about an early death. Zoe said,

> I am aware that life is so short, and I have to make the
> most of it. I worry at times, that something could happen
> to my husband or myself, and my daughter would be
> without a parent. I don't want her to ever go through what
> I did as a child.

Vi said that the possibility of an early death is a constant thought
in her life. Like the others, her greatest concern is that her children
could experience her own childhood loss:

> That's hard for me [going out on a date with my husband]
> because I'm leaving my kids. Every time we go out the
> door without them, I'm afraid we're going to get killed in
> a car accident, and I think about leaving our children alone
> without parents. I know that's stupid, but I feel that way.

Notice the words that these women selected in their descriptions:
afraid, worry, leaving, alone. These are feelings shaped by their
parent's death. They are also feelings that they would like their children to avoid—at least by parental death. Adults who expressed these
feelings indicated that such thinking is not necessarily reasonable.

Fears for the future may also involve the possible loss of other
significant persons in one's life. Having already experienced the
traumatic event of parental death, one would rather not endure
other, permanent separations. For many, this fear begins in childhood, with the fear of losing the surviving parent. Isabel described a
moment in which she feared the death of her father: "I remember,
when I was in seventh grade, I got a phone call. My dad had an
accident at work. My first thought was, 'He's dead.' For years... the
thought of my father dying was a huge worry for me." Vi also
described this childhood fear, which she admitted transferring to
her husband and children:

> One of the immediate affects was a fear of loss of some-
> one else in my life. My mom would go to orchestra

concerts and Wednesday night practices. She was supposed to be home at midnight. If it was five minutes after midnight, I was immediately crying, sobbing, praying. I was afraid she got killed in a car accident or something happened to her. It was a tremendous fear. Then I transferred that to my husband…Now it's my husband, the kids, or myself. When my husband says that he has a headache or the worst headache he's ever had, I jump to the worst conclusions…I'm always waiting for the next bombshell to fall. It's something that I have to constantly fight and reason out in my mind and say, "Listen, there's no logical reason why you have to fear that this is going to happen to you again—just because it happened to you when you were a child." I don't want to have to go through it again or have anyone I love experience that either.

Vi said that she is waiting for the *next* bombshell to fall. The first bombshell was the death of her father when she was twelve years-old. She knows that with the unpredictability of life, another bombshell can fall on her life at any time. Vi recognized that this fear is the biggest influence of her loss.

Hopes for the Future

Persons living with the childhood loss of a parent may also live with a constant hope to live to a specific stage of life, which does not necessarily include the age of their parent's death. Many start with a certain stage, then move to another stage, and then to another, having a fluctuating, minimum age as their goal. As Oscar said, "That was my dream—'If I'm going to die, I want to die after my kids are minimum, out of high school.' Then when they started out of high school I would say, 'Minimum, after college.' " Chad expressed a similar progression in his hopes:

I can remember when my oldest child was five and I would just look at her and pray that God would grant me enough years that I would see her graduate from high school and get married...because I know the pain of losing a parent when you are young, and I didn't want my kids to have to go through that.

Laura also had a minimum age requirement: "I always wanted to be able to live long enough to see my kids grow up and just see the grand kids." Vi said that she wants to live at least until her children are officially adults: "I start playing deals with God. I say, 'Just let me live until they're eighteen.'"

Living More Deliberately

Individuals living with the early death of a parent may also prepare more deliberately for the future. This involves making choices in life that impact the lives of other people. Most of the adults who described this aspect of their lives were also parents. Another chapter will explore adults' understandings of the impact of their loss on family planning. In this section, the emphasis is a very brief example of adults' preparations for the future as an outgrowth of their awareness of mortality.

Irwin seemed very proud of the fact that he has been very expressive in the love that he has shown his family. He related this drive to the loss of his father when he was fifteen years old. About his personal determination, Irwin said, "I made a deliberate stance in my life—that I'm not going to leave this world without telling people that I love them." Chuck described his desire to invest in his children: "I wouldn't say that I'm being overprotective of my kids, but being very aware...If I have to choose between doing this activity without them or doing this activity with them, I would choose doing the activity with them. It's an awareness." Chad related his deliberateness in parenting to his awareness of mortality:

I think of deliberateness, consciousness, being aware of "Am I spending enough time with my kids?" Feeling like it's a delicate thing. It's not a given that I'm going to be around to see them another birthday or another

Christmas. Those things aren't guaranteed, and you realize this when you lose a parent at a young age. I really wanted to make the most of the time.

Sam said, "Love your spouse. Love your kids. You just don't know when one of them is going to be gone. You're just *here* a short time."

Summary

What does it mean to live with the loss of a parent who died in childhood or adolescence? It means that one has a constant awareness of mortality. From this awareness comes more specific understandings: an awareness that death can happen at any time; an awareness of approaching the deceased parent's age of death; the formation of hopes and fears for the futures; and a drive to live more deliberately. As Sam said, "I plan like I'm going to be here a long time...but I could...go quick."

These feelings are not simply a knowledge of the basic facts of life and death. These facts have a greater awareness attached to them; they involve a deep, primordial awareness of death. Most people know that diseases and accidents can strike at anytime, but does everyone prepare for the possibility of death? When do people live life more deliberately? It is often seen in the lives of those that have faced, or are facing, the possibility of death. How many surviving heart-attack victims live life more deliberately? How many life-threatening illness and accident survivors feel a greater sense of living and the need to be prepared for death? When children or adolescents experience the death of a parent, they feel a greater sense of death's imminence, which stays with them into adulthood.

Personal Insights

A constant awareness of mortality, as a result of experiencing the early deaths of our fathers, exists in both my wife and me. How this awareness translates into our family life varies. We believe that our loss has helped us to have a strong sense of family togetherness.

My wife's father died in a car accident when he was thirty-three years old and she was twelve. She has passed his age of death, but the possibility of a sudden ending to life is always in the back of her mind. Although we leave our children to go on a retreat or date, it is always with the possibility that we could die. She knows that God will take care of our children, just as He took care of us in the absence of our fathers; but as described by those interviewed for this book, Wendy does not want our children to endure the same pain.

Pastoral ministry is filled with expectations to be away from children, but Wendy and I are very selective in what we choose to attend. Although Wendy's concerns involve the possibility of tragedy, we simply do not see the need to be away from our children. For me, I weigh each event against being home with my family, and I'd rather be with my family. For the enrichment of our marriage, Wendy and I go out on dates and attend an annual marriage-enrichment conference. Other than that, we are together as a family. A man recently said to me, "You not only encourage parents to be family-focused and deliberate in child-rearing, but you model it with your own life and family. Thank you." That was one of the highest compliments that I have ever received. I believe that our loss has helped us to see that there is nothing more important than loving and being with our family.

I have not yet approached the age of my father's death, but I am not very concerned about it. My awareness of mortality has translated into deliberate living. Since I may be gone at anytime, I must make the most of every day. I must make my children aware of my love and pride for them; I must impress Biblical principles upon them; I must create positive memories for them. I not only talk to my children, but I regularly write to them. Many of the notes and letters that I have written to my children are ones that they will not read until they are much older. I am planning to give the letters to them in person, but I know that I have no guarantee. My loss has prompted me to parent my children in such a way that if I should die, they would clearly know of my love for them. They will always have my written words.

For the Surviving Parent

- **Children need to know that their surviving parent is safe.** Children of early parent death have learned that life is unpredictable. They want to hold fast to their only living parent, and they may exhibit fear when their surviving parent goes somewhere without them. Surviving parent should make sure that the children always know where they are and how they can be contacted. The surviving parent should especially never leave the house in anger or frustration.
- **Children need to know that their surviving parent is healthy.** Take care of your health and assure your children that you are healthy. Communicate with them about doctor's appointments, health concerns, etc. On the other hand, be careful not to add more fear to minds, which are already aware that their other parent could die.
- **Children need to know what will happen to them if you die.** Make a will and let children know that they would be in the care of loving people. If you have not taken these steps, you may want to involve them in the process.
- **Children should be encouraged to think of living a long life.** The early death of a parent creates another notable date in history that occurs many years after the death. Children may wonder if they will also die at the age at which their parent died. This may be unavoidable in some children, but all children can be encouraged to think about living a long life.
- **Children can understand living more deliberately.** Children have learned that life is unpredictable and fragile. They can be encouraged to use these already-learned lessons to be more deliberate in the ways that they show love to others, especially their family members. This must be done sensitively, so as to not make them more fearful of the death of loved ones.

....

O DEATH, WHERE IS YOUR VICTORY?
O DEATH, WHERE IS YOUR STING?
1 Corinthians 15:55

Chapter 6

Absence of the Parent Throughout the Remainder of Life

When a tourist, especially in a foreign land, experiences the loss of a tour guide, the absence of the tour guide is immediately felt. As the tourist continues the journey of growing into an experienced traveler, the absence of the tour guide continues to be felt. The traveler misses the tour guide, specific moments with the tour guide, and the future that never was—nor will be. The tour guide was not present as the tourist grew into an experienced traveler—absent during the milestones of the journey—absent when advice was desired along the journey. Even as an experienced traveler of many years, the individual may want to seek the wisdom of a more-experienced tour guide. One may find a substitute tour guide from which to glean wisdom, but it does not change the fact that the absence of the original tour guide continues to be felt, as he or she cannot be replaced.

Absence, a main theme of this experience, can be defined, "The state of not being present."[1] In order to adequately understand the significance of absence, it is important to understand presence: "The existence of a person or thing in a certain place."[2] The person is the parent, and the "certain place" is in the life of that parent's child. Presence is also described: "attendance or company; immediate vicinity, close proximity."[3] Following a parent's death, his or her attendance, company, vicinity, and proximity are not physically possible—ever again. They are absent.

Living with the loss experienced through the death of a parent in childhood or adolescence means that one feels the absence of a parent throughout life. The presence of that parent is absent from the life of the child, youth, and adult forever. Quinn described it this way: "There's an empty spot on the bed. There is an empty chair at the table. There is an empty newspaper laid over a face. However you want to depict it, it's *gone*." He also described this finality of the loss in contrast to the absence of a father that has not died:

> There might be a daddy that left home; he's still out there somewhere; he could call; he could show up; he could write you a letter. But if a dad's dead—he's gone. It's over. You're not gonna hear another voice. You're not gonna see another thing. You're not gonna get another hug. You're not gonna feel another touch...There's a difference when it's over and done and gone, and you can't even touch anything but a tombstone.

Missing the parent is disclosed in longing. Sam mentioned a longing for his absent father: "It's just always a longing there for him, and he just wasn't there." Longing is defined as, "prolonged, unceasing, or earnest desire."[4] The absence of presence is a felt reality; the parent's presence is gone forever. As Chad said, "When you lose something, you realize what you've lost." One can only remember, long, or fantasize about the presence of a parent that they will not see, touch, or hear again on this earth. Brooke said, "It is difficult to explain, but it's almost like a part of yourself is missing."

Missing the Parent

A person can miss the presence of another individual, but the absence of a parent in the life of a child is a uniquely felt loss. Isabel said, "The love of a mother is not replaceable." As Laura explained, "You can never recoup what you've lost." Missing the parent is an essential feature of the experience, disclosed in two different ways: missing the person and missing the parental figure. Most individuals miss both the person and the parental figure, as indicated by their descriptions of missing "my mom" and "a mom." Others may remember a deceased parent who was abusive or distant. Still others may have no memory of their deceased parent. In either case, those without specific, positive recollections feel the absence of a parental figure more than the absence of a person. As Billie said, "Since I didn't remember my mother, I didn't miss her as a person." Her words illustrate the difference between feeling the absence of a specific individual and feeling the absence of a parental figure.

A Person

Missing a parent, as part of this lived experience, involves missing a specific person. Of his mother, Chad said, "I think I absolutely took her for granted growing up...She was just there...When I lost her, then I realized just what an impact she had and how important she was to me."

Quincey described how she felt the absence of her mother during her pregnancy and the delivery of her daughter:

> My pregnancy was emotionally difficult. I couldn't ask my mom what it was like for her. I didn't have her there to help. She would never get to see her granddaughter. All of this made for quite a bit of stress. Day to day I am fine. I enjoy my life and my loving family, but I still miss her.

Missing her mother points to a longing for a particular person for whom there is no substitute.

Belinda spoke in appreciation of her mother-in-law, but recognized that her mother's presence could not be replaced: "I longed for my real mother. My husband's mother actually came to spend time with us after our first child was born... I appreciate her lots, but she is not like a mother to me." Amy lost her mother when she was only two months old, yet she recalled longing for her: "I have wondered what she was like and I heard that she sang a lot... She laughed a lot and was a very cheerful person, I guess. It made me long to know her."

In expressions of missing the deceased parent, most adults make clear reference to a specific person by using the word "my." Instead of missing *a* father or mother, they longed for a specific father or mother—their own. Brooke began referring to a father, but ended with a reference to her father: "Whenever I feel threatened, lonely, or afraid it's like I revert back to that 'poor, ten-year-old little girl that lost her Daddy'....... I will always miss my Father." Vi's statement illustrates the same longing for her own father:

> When we go to Grandma's house to visit, what would it be like to have my dad there? I can't even fathom what that would be like. To get together on Thanksgiving or to come and watch the kids at their Christmas program; to call when I'm worried about something because I need him to encourage me and pray with me? That part will never exist. I'll never know that.

Vi also recognized that she will always live with the absence of her father, as will her children. Quincey expressed a combination between missing the presence of her mother and knowing that she will always live with her absence:

> Living without my mom is like being immortal but starving to death. The pain never ends and it really never abates...I have not learned to live with it and I don't think I ever will... It does mean that with every happy moment, there will be pain. With every joyous occasion, there will be sadness. It will always be like this because she is not here.

A Parental Figure

Adults who experienced the early death of a parent also describe the missing presence of *a* mother or *a* father. They miss the presence or function of a parental figure. One participant shared this story about herself and a relative, who also experienced the death of his father:

> It was Father's Day, or the day before, and a girl asked us, "I don't know what to get my father. What would you get yours?" We both looked at each other like, "Well, we have no idea. We don't even know what that's like at this point."

It was not the absence of a specific person that was described. Rather, it was the absence of *a* father.

The absence of a parental role may be felt when one is cast into assuming the responsibilities of the role. For example, Rhonda said, "My sister was only ten years old; so suddenly I felt like I had to be her mom…taking over that role and helping her…that's so hard to do as a sibling, because while you're trying to help her, you're still fighting with her and being a normal kid." Amidst needing a mother, Rhonda filled a motherly role for her sister.

The absence of a parent may also be felt at moments that are reserved especially for a father or mother. Like many boys, Chuck missed the presence of a father at his sporting events: "Sports was a big deal for me… Having a parent involved to practice with you or being involved as a coach—whatever—there was that void." Nancy remembered: "All those traditional things in school where you bring your mom…I was always borrowing a parent of somebody. That probably was the greatest difficulty of not having a parent there." Kathy spoke of the missing presence of a father in her life, which she felt in the past and feels in the present: "I feel the extreme loss of father. I didn't have a daddy and I have this extreme loss that I can't have it now… I didn't have a dad in my twenties and thirties and forties."

As seen in the previous descriptions, the absence of someone in a parental position—a parental role—a person who served the function of being a parent—is a felt reality in the lives of adults who experienced the early death of a parent. Whether a person has positive memories, negative memories, or no memories, they feel the absence of having a mother or father.

Can individuals miss a deceased parent of whom they have only negative memories? Can individuals miss a deceased parent of whom they have no memories? The answer to both questions is, "Yes." Each adult with this life experience feels the absence of a parent, but not every adult misses the presence of a specific individual.

Missing Specific Moments with the Parent

Whereas the previous section included descriptions of feeling the absence of a deceased parent, this section includes ways in which one may miss specific moments with the parent—specific moments that never did and never will occur. Moments in which a parent is needed or desired are moments that stir up feelings of disappointment and cause the absence of the parent to be felt again.

Special Occasions

Special occasions are the most prominent moments in which individuals feel the absence of their deceased parent. Such special occasions are often recognized as the milestones of life. Chad said, It was hard dealing with the loss, and then I think it was hard after—her not being there for graduation—her not seeing me graduate from college—her not seeing me get married to Molly, who I grew up with next door. She always kind of knew we would get married anyway. It's always all of those major events—I always missed having her there—having the first child and knowing she would've been a great grandma...but my kids never get to know her. Those are all really, really tough things.

Alice expressed a similar outlook:

My high school graduation; college graduation; post graduate graduation—I wanted him there for all of them... Three big experiences...First, my wedding day. I wanted him to walk me down the aisle, and even though I appreciated my mother doing it and supporting me, I felt deprived. I experience that sadness when I watch someone else walked down the aisle by her father. Another very strong sense of loss was with the birth of my first child, my son Brandon. I wanted my dad to be a part of that. When I found out I was pregnant, my husband and I went to my father's grave to talk about it and celebrate that his little girl was having her first child. That was very healing for me.

Individuals not only feel the absence of a parent before and after a milestone event, but they may also feel conscious of the absence while at the height of the moment. Mike said, "When I was standing up at my marriage, I just thought…'I wish my mom was here to experience this.'" A similar scenario was expressed by Brooke, who lost her father at the age of ten:

I still miss my Father and I think about him all the time. I remember how I cried when I got married, and I wasn't crying because I was happy; I was crying because I wished my Father could have been there to see me. I also thought about him when I graduated from high school; when both of his parents died; when my mother almost died once; when my sister had both of her children…

There is no question that milestone events are a major part of feeling the absence of a parent's presence. As Mike said, "But those key moments—it always comes back up—it creeps back up." The loss creeps back up when life reaches milestones; the absence becomes quite noticeable.

What is it about the milestone events that makes them such prominent moments in feeling the absence of a parent? Milestone events usually signify a passage of great change and great significance. For example, single life and married life are separated by a wedding. Being a student and a graduate are separated by graduation. Being childless and being a parent is separated by the event of childbirth. These can be deeply felt transforming moments in life.

As noted throughout the world in countless cultures, being human includes passages of growth and change. Many individuals prefer to share these passages of life with those to whom they are most profoundly connected—often those who are responsible for one's own birth and upbringing. For some, it is like receiving a validation to go on with the next phase of life. It may also be a way for an individual to feel that he or she is fulfilling the desires and dreams of the previous generation. Human beings are involved in rituals in which parents and children—older and younger—are present. Without a parent's presence at such times, absence is more obvious.

Every-day Moments

Along with the milestone events, individuals may feel the absence of their parent within the every-day moments of life—the "normal stuff" of life, such as the casual conversations between a parent and child. Irene, now in her twenties, experienced the death of her mother at the age of eleven. More than ten years after her mother's death, Irene said that she misses the sharing of every-day aspects of life with her mother:

> That is what I miss the most, in some strange way: sitting around the table and talking about unimportant things at supper and just feeling that connection. I so want that connection...I realize just how short of a time I had with my mother. How much I could give to just do the simple things, such as arguing about clothes, music, and my hair color. I long for those mundane aspects of life.

Most adults who mentioned the every-day moments said that the lack of conversation with the deceased parent is a felt absence. Sam is very involved in his sons' lives. At times while being with them, he has thought about the absence of those moments in his own life—times in which he could not and can not share with his father:

> I always think, "It would have been nice if I would have had these types of memories with my dad."... There's

never been any particular time where I've said, "You know, I wish I had a dad." It's just been there all the way along—just little things—the every-day things that my sons take for granted, and I'm just here.

The last three words in Sam's quote, "I'm just here," are filled with much meaning. A parent is gone—not *here*. It is in the every-day living that adults have wanted their parents to be *here*. Many adults, knowing what it's like to not have a parent *here*, chose to be *there* for their own children. Such every-day living involves a number of activities that most people may take for granted.

Difficult Times

Absence may also be felt in relation to difficult times. In difficult moments, people want or need the presence of others to whom they are profoundly connected. Chris acknowledged,

When do you need your mother most? Whenever that is, that is when you miss her the most…Is it on the day you find out that your pregnancy is not going well? Or is it on the day you start into labor, more than seven weeks early, after a very stressful six months of wondering if your son would even survive?

Olivia spoke of the absence of her father in the past challenges in her own life: "I have always felt that if my Dad had been around, somehow maybe that awful period in my life would have been more bearable. We are taught that a father's child-rearing always includes protection." Olivia expressed an assumption—a hope—that the presence of her dad would have protected her from difficult times. She explained, "My youngest brother is an alcoholic and how I wish my Father was here to help him… Not having a parent at such difficult times in our lives has been hard."

The absence of the deceased parent may also be felt in connection to general difficulty in life. Irene said, "It's the steady accumulation of little things—a little heartbreak there—a tear here. No one around me understands this at all... Just to have her here." She alluded to the fact that one can be helped to face challenges by having a parent's presence. Vi spoke of a similar desire for comfort that she could seek from her father if he was alive:

> Mainly now, at this stage in my life, it's wishing I had a spiritual parent to go to—someone to whom I could say, "Daddy, my husband, or one of the kids, isn't feeling good. Could you please pray for him?" I don't have a parent that I can call on for that part. That's so important.

In times of difficulty, one may desire the help of someone who has more life experience or wisdom. The absence of a parent means that the parent is not available to be present in every-day moments; to share joyous occasions; or to give advice in times of difficulty. One who lives with this early loss has no such opportunity with his or her deceased parent. The person can only wonder how that parent may have been involved in his or her life or what advice that parent would have given.

Missing a Future with the Parent

Can individuals miss something that has not happened? Can individuals feel the absence of something that they never knew? Can individuals long for something that they will never have? The individual who lives with the early loss of a parent may also feel the absence of his or her parent in what-would-have-come-to-be.

Frozen in Time

New memories of a deceased parent cannot be created after the parent has died. Beyond the day of death, there was no change in the parent and no opportunities to create memories. Time continues for everyone except the deceased parent. Nancy said of her mother,

> She's kind of frozen at age forty-eight or younger...The other day we calculated out age. It's kind of strange to

think how active she would be. Would she go shopping for prom dresses? That kind of thing—you just never know.

As indicated by Nancy, the deceased parent is frozen in time. New pictures cannot be added to the family photo album. New pictures cannot be stored in memory.

Having a parent for many years provides many more memories for an individual. Persons who experienced the early death of a parent in childhood or adolescence have a very limited range of memories to recall. They had few years between the emergence of memory in childhood and the death of the parent. With the parent frozen in time, these persons will never know what the parent would have looked like and what new memories would have been created. The parent is frozen in time.

Adult Relationship

Living with the early death of a parent means that a child does not have the possibility of having an adult relationship with his or her parent. Knowing a parent, adult-to-adult, is an opportunity that many people take for granted. Those living with this loss will never have such a relationship with their deceased parent. When most children become adults, they continue to be the children of a parent. A transition into adult status takes place, but a parent-child relationship still exists. Sam said, "I would have liked to have that...I never made that transition with my dad."

This aspect of absence is about what-will-never-be and would-have-been-nice-to-have. Chad said, You become an adult and you understand what adults think. You understand what adults go through. You'd like to be able to communicate on an adult level. Having those kind of insights of your parents—not just being a mom or not just being a dad, but being a person… It would've been so nice to talk to her about her history… and what she thinks about politics. It would've been nice to have gotten to know her as an adult… She would've been a really interesting person to get to know, not just as a mom to a little kid.

Vi also described the absence of an adult-to-adult relationship that she will never have with her father:

> One thing that is the hardest is that I realize, that as a child, I never really knew who my father was...as a person. Was he gentle? Was he kind? Was he funny? Was he tender hearted toward people? Was he welcoming? How did he treat people? I don't know. I don't remember. I mean, I know he was very well liked and very friendly. I never remember any unkind things that he did, but I just don't know who he was. What kind of jokes did he like to laugh at? Those who lose a parent in adulthood have so much more to say about who their parent was as a person—not just what they did, but they really knew them.

Persons living with this loss would have liked to combine their adult understanding with knowing their deceased parent. What is it like to know your parent when you are an adult? Those who experience the early death of a parent will never know their parent in this way. As seen in Vi's words, there are many questions about the deceased parent that cannot be answered.

Grandparenting

Those who experience the early death of a parent will never observe their deceased parent become a grandparent. This is another aspect of felt absence—another way in which the parent's death created a void in life. It is a loss for themselves, their children, and their deceased parent. As adults spoke of absence in the lives of their children, they were also speaking of their own felt absence. Not having a grandmother or grandfather for one's child is another way in which life continues to feel incomplete.

Mike experienced the death of his mother at age thirteen. He is now in his thirties and has a two-year-old son. He is reminded of the loss of "grandma" when he observes his mother-in-law with his son: "Maybe I'm envious of my mother-in-law–that she's getting to spend time with her grandson, and my mom's not. Once in a while I'm thinking, "That should be my mom being able to get to do that."

Mike used the word "should," signifying a common expectation in life—that a parent "should be" or "should have been" a grandparent. People assume that their parents will become grandparents; the culture shows this progression, and individuals expect it.

Just as Mike described his feelings, prompted by something he observed, other adults also recount the times in which they feel their loss while observing others. For Vi, a reminder of the loss is felt when she observes friends and their fathers:

> I would love for my kids to have a grandpa. Mainly, that comes too when I see other friends my age and their relationships with their fathers. I'll be thinking, "Wow. How neat it is that this woman has a Daddy still alive and her kids have grandpas." I think that's probably where it hits me the most right now.

Zoe said, "Sometimes when I pick her up at school, I see the other children's grandparents picking up their grandchildren and a pang of sadness goes through my heart. But I move on. My daughter never knew my father."

What if the child never knew the missing grandparent? Chad said, "I think there's a sense of loss there, that somehow our kids lost a valuable opportunity to have that relationship." Adults also recognized that their children's loss is not necessarily a loss felt by the children. For example, Laura said, "I think about the difference that a grandparent could have made in their lives...something that they missed, but which they probably don't miss at all. I don't know, but I miss for them." Her last four words in this statement are very interesting. Possibly, she remembers the joy of being close to a grandparent. At the same time, she knows that her children will not have that. Her children probably don't miss that relationship, since they never had it, but Laura misses it for them. Vi elaborated on the same issue. She recognized that her children may not miss that relationship now, in their younger years, but they may feel an absence when they notice that others have such a relationship:

> They don't understand that though. Maybe, when they get

older they'll understand it more. When they see other people with their grandpas, and then they will realize that they don't have that. They will also realize that our family is not "normal" when it comes to family relationships with grandpas...We feel the need to fill in the missing gaps with being a close knit family ourselves.

Is the loss really a loss for the children of those who experienced the early death of a parent? Although adults recognized that their children may not feel the absence of a deceased grandparent, there exists the dynamic of wanting one's child to know that the deceased parent was and is greatly valued. On the other hand, those who have experienced this loss do not want to create unnecessary heartache in the lives of their children, over someone who their children will never know. As one participant indicated, children may feel a sense of loss when they observe the bond between grandparents and grandchildren. Then again, if children have other grandparents in their lives, the loss may not be felt. However, such a scenario does not mean that the loss is diminished in the life of the individual who lost the parent.

What was initially a childhood loss became a life-long loss. According to a number of adults, the early death of a parent becomes a loss for the next generation. Whether it is felt by the next generation or not, the "middle" generation feels that it is.

Summary

What is it like to live with the death of a parent which occurred in childhood or adolescence? It means that one feels the absence of the parent throughout life. The absence is felt in missing the parent; missing specific times with the parent; missing the future with the parent. In adulthood, the loss continues to exist as the loss of a parent, and it may also be felt as the loss of a would-be grandparent.

The event of death has taken place; the early years in the loss are passed; childhood and adolescence are gone. Following these time periods is the adult life in which the reverberations of the loss are recognized in the felt absence of the deceased parent.

Personal Insights

When my dad died, I was thirteen years old, an age at which I had just started to learn many new things from him. I went fishing with him in my younger years, but I had just begun to be interested in learning about fishing. I also became a licensed hunter. My dad was a man who enjoyed the outdoors, and I was beginning to share his enjoyment. As a bricklayer, he was also a good handyman who could build and fix many things. He could fix his truck, build a house, tile a bathroom, and more. When my dad died, so did my opportunities to learn his skills and enjoyments.

He would have been there to teach me about the outdoors, show me how to fix my car, and help me build or remodel a house. I am not much of an outdoorsman, but I have often wished that someone would teach me. I do not know much about cars, so I hire mechanics, except for changing the oil, which is something he taught to me. As a homeowner, I am forced to learn how to fix and build things, but it would be so much easier if my dad were here to teach me.

My dad and I both enjoyed football, as most people in Western Pennsylvania did, but he died before I played in high school. I only played for one year because I had a difficult time with a coach that never offered encouragement. I am convinced that if my dad had been alive, he would have provided the balance that I needed to continue playing.

I once heard a story about a teenage quarterback who experienced the death of his blind father. A few days after his father's death the young quarterback was expected to lead his team in the championship game. The coach excused him from the game, but the teenager wanted to play. His performance was incredible—the best he had ever played. After the game, the coach asked him, "What happened out there? That was the greatest game you've ever played." The boy said, "Coach, my dad was a Christian, and I know he's in heaven. Today was the first day that he could watch me play football." This story touched my heart, because I knew what it was like to experience the death of a father while also knowing that he was in heaven.

Other specific moments of missing him are fresh in my mind. They are mixed with a great love for my mother, who attended a number of my events alone. I missed him at my track meets, especially when other fathers were there; I missed him when I hit a grand slam in an all-star game; I missed him in the front row of the auditorium when I performed as a lead in a high school musical; I missed him at my high school graduation; I missed him in the driveway as I drove off to go to college for the first time; I missed him when I brought Wendy home for the first time; I missed him at our wedding; I missed him at each of my college graduations; and I missed him at the birth of each of our children.

I continue to miss him, more than twenty years after his death, but now I miss him for my children. I also miss Wendy's dad, although I did not have the privilege of meeting him. I missed him in the life events that we have shared—especially at our wedding, when Wendy walked down the isle by herself. I also miss him as an influence in the lives of our children. Both of these godly men would have enriched our children's lives in ways that we can only imagine. People say, "You don't miss what you've never had," but we know that our children are missing something valuable. I wish that they knew their grandfathers well enough to refer to them as "grandpa," but without a relationship they usually refer to them as, "Daddy's dad" or "Mommy's dad." We lost our fathers, and they lost their grandfathers. Wendy and I cherish our memories of our godly grandfathers, but our children are not able to have such memories of their grandfathers.

For the Surviving Parent

- **Children may always miss their parent.** Each adult, interviewed for this book, miss having *a* parent, but most of them miss *their own* parent. This is another way in which the permanency of their loss is felt. The missing continues through life as the individual does not stop being their parent's child.
- **Christian children should be taught these foundational truths:** Jesus is always with them; Sad and lonely feelings repre-

sent opportunities to pray; Their surviving parent and entire family will depend on God for comfort and help.

- **Christian children can be assured that they will have the opportunity to see their Christian parent again.** There is more to life than living and dying. The deceased parent met Jesus face-to-face and is at the start of eternal life. Thank God that children can be given this hope. Christians know no permanent good-byes!

- **Children may not accept a stepparent as a replacement parent.** This statement is not meant to discourage the surviving parent from marrying again. A loving stepparent may be exactly what a child needs—a person who will become a father-figure or mother-figure. While a stepparent often becomes *a* father or mother to your children, they may never become *the* father or mother.

- **Children want to know that the surviving parent misses the deceased.** The surviving parent should communicate with his or her children about the ways in which the deceased spouse is missed. Children may be surprised to find out that they share similar thoughts with their parent. In this endeavor, the surviving parent may also help them to appreciate things that they have not yet pondered.

- **Children should be encouraged to recognize their parent at milestones.** Families should celebrate life-events with acknowledgement of the deceased. In the early years, children need the surviving parent to take the lead in this. In later years, they will need to know that such recognition is still welcome.

....

He will wipe away every tear from their eyes;
and there will no longer be any death;
there will no longer be any mourning, or crying, or pain;
the first things have passed away."
Revelation 21:4

Chapter 7

Presence of the Parent in Memory throughout the Remainder of Life

W hen a tourist experiences the loss of a tour guide, he or she is forced to continue traveling without that guide for the remainder of the journey. Memories of the tour guide are often held in high value, since the tour guide will never be present again. Many memories remain vivid as the tourist reviews them in his or her travels. Other memories fade with time as the tourist continues the journey, which produces it's own memories. Similar to a person who searches a computer database, the tourist may search his or her memories of the tour guide in order to make a decision or solve a problem.

While traveling, the tourist remembers the tour guide through various associations, such as sights, sounds, and smells. A variety of items, people, and places serve as triggers to memories that surface throughout the journey. Memories of the tour guide and memories of the brief time in which they traveled together may also surface at unexpected moments.

Tourists may enjoy sharing memories of the absent tour guide with others. They may learn of another person's recollections of the tour guide. They may also share their memories with the tourists who they will guide in the future. In any case, the absent tour guide remains present in memory.

Although the parent is absent, a connection to the deceased parent remains. It is not a corporal presence, but a memory of presence. When presence is absent, then the alternative is to hold on to a memory—a residue of past presence.

A child depends upon a parent as a tour guide through a strange land. In most cases, the parent is the object of stability, wisdom, and survival. When the parent is gone, assumptions and expectations often die with the parent. A parent's death signifies the end of life as it was known. From the point of death, a new life begins. The former life is not erased from existence, but it is remembered.

Persons, who experience the early death of a parent, speak of the importance of having memories. Quinn stressed the value that he has placed on memories:

> I can lose pictures. We lost our house to fire. You can lose that. You can't take these memories from me... I was a fireman for four years, so I know. The things I see people looking for are not their pictures, not their Bible, and not the important papers. They're looking for family.

Living with this loss means living with memories and depending on memories as a way to stay connected to one's parent; connected to life before the loss; connected to part of self that is gone forever.

Retaining and Losing Memories

Most recollections of the deceased parent are burned into memory forever. Others fade with time. Disappointment occurs when memories, which may be few, begin to fade.

Retaining memories is a way to retain a hint of a parent's presence. Kim explained, "My mother is not physically alive, but her memory is very much alive with me. I still can feel her attitudes and love with me. I think that there are so many similarities between us that I remind myself of her." In her case, the memory of her mother will always be with her because she resembles her recollections of her mother.

Similar to photographs in photo albums, memories include those "snapshots" of remembered moments. Irwin, who experienced the death of his father fifty-five years ago, said, "I would say that the pictures are as vivid now as they were back then." Zac said, "I guess most of the stuff I just visualize myself." Similar to revisiting a painting on a wall or a photograph in an album, many adults retain vividness of certain memories because they have revisited them many times over the years. As Kathy expressed, "I think that when you've revisited a situation, it keeps it fresh in your mind because you haven't allowed those cells in your brain to forget it."

The vividness retained in memories can also be due to the nature of the moment. For many individuals, the memory is of a milestone event with the parent or the last "good-bye." Zoe recalled, "He hadn't been feeling well that day and was sitting in the living room with my mother when I kissed him goodnight and told him I hoped he felt better tomorrow. 'I hope so too, honey,' were the last words he ever said to me." Irene remembered, "My mother has been gone for twelve years, this April, and in some ways it seems like so long ago. In other ways, it seems like yesterday. I can still remember the look on her face the day she died." About her father Olivia said, "I can still see his face and hear his voice just like it was yesterday."

The fading of good memories can be another aspect of loss. Cynthia expressed her frustration with not remembering: "It makes me sad when memories fade...My mother's been dead for twenty-three years, and I just can't remember things as clearly." Quincey said that the fading hurts: "I've forgotten her smell and her laugh, and that really hurts." Billie said:

> When I was little, I thought I remembered a few things about her, but as time went on, that faded, and I honestly don't remember one thing about her. I find that very sad, since I love my son so much; and the thought that he wouldn't have remembered me, I always found very sad.

Living with the loss of a parent who died in childhood or adolescence means that a portion of the growing-up years and all of the adult years are without new memories of the parent. Why is this important? Memories serve as a way to stay connected to the parent. When memories fade, connection dissipates. Therefore, the fading of memories can be an added loss—a loss of something that cannot be regained. Vi said: "The feeling of him fades. The feelings of remembering him fades—day-dreaming of him—wishing—stuff like that...That fades. Memories keep going, but they are the same memories. No new ones usually pop up." Keeping memories of a deceased parent's presence becomes a challenge for some, especially when memories are not recalled with the same frequency.

Remembering the Parent Through Associations

One way that a parent remains present in the memory of individuals is by way of associations. Associations are helpful to recall memories of the deceased parent, who was lost many years ago. Such associations serve as triggers that help one to remember.

Vi explained that most memories of her father need a trigger: "They are based on people saying things, or if I look at pictures. It is usually a trigger that pops them up. I don't just think of them for no reason at all." She also described an example:

> I can remember any picture that he's in...The pictures help bring back memories of certain situations. I associate everything that way... Memories don't last forever. If I want to remember him, I like to sit and look at pictures. Then I remember more stories and situations.

Objects

One of the most common ways to retain memories of the deceased parent is through a tangible object. The object is not always an expensive item, but it may be a memento that most others would define as "junk." Such an object can serve as a springboard to specific memories of a parent. On the other hand, they may remind the beholder of a parent's presence without actually prompting a specific memory.

In most cases, a possession does not produce a specific memory, but it serves as a way to remember the deceased parent in a very general way. Zac explained,

> I have my father's jewelry box...I remember liking to look through the stuff when I was a kid...Just some miscellaneous stuff...They don't give me memories of him specifically. It just gives me a memory of having him *there*. That was his stuff and I liked it. It doesn't make me think of any specific time or give me a picture of his face.

As disclosed in Zac's experience, tangible objects can simply give one "a memory of having him there." As was discussed in the previous chapter about absence, the word "there" signifies presence. Where is there? It is in one's presence. Zac's father is absent, but he is present in memory. Objects help remembering to happen.

Samples of the deceased parent's written word are among those items that adults value. Chad said, "She wrote a lot of letters. She wrote a lot of poems during those years when she was struggling..." Through the letters, he felt like he was able to learn about her strength. Nancy has a few mementos, but most meaningful to her is her mother's writings: "Other things that I've gotten have been through friends and relatives who have sent them to me, like letters. That's probably more important to me than having something." Rhonda said of her mother's writings: "She was composing a lot of poetry, and my dad put together a book of it in her memory... That really showed a lot of her true colors...There were a lot of personal things about her..." Similar to the value that Chad placed on his mother's writings, Rhonda also appreciated this way to know what her mother was like.

These written items may be the type of keepsake that most individuals with this loss would want to have. It seems that such a keepsake may provide the most accurate way of knowing more about the deceased parent. In various forms of written expression, especially journals and diaries, writers expose themselves by revealing what is inside—their deepest feelings, thoughts, dreams, and struggles. The reader of such writings can get a sense of the writer's strength and character. For individuals who have grown up not knowing a parent, a parent's personal writings are a treasure.

The importance of items is increased with the meanings attached to them. Vi plays her father's viola. After he died, she decided to teach herself to play it and continue his music heritage:

> I grew up being taught how to play the violin, and my dad always played the viola. When he died, I took his viola and taught myself how to play it. I'm actually very good at it, and I've gotten lots of compliments on it. Part of me never wants that part to stop. I feel that my music heritage is from him...That's who he was.

Vi's viola is more than just a reminder of her father. As she said, "That's who he was." He was a musician and a violist. He was the only one who played that viola; It was part of him. With it, she carries on his instrument, talent, heritage, and musical characteristics.

The items are intriguing, but even more fascinating are the meanings which adults attach to them. Many items may be of little worth to anyone else. To the owners, these items are much more than material possessions. They are associations to the deceased parent; items which are purposely kept as connections to the general memory and specific memories.

Senses

Sights and sounds are among the most common associations to memories of the deceased parent. By seeing something or hearing a sound, one can recall memories of a parent';;s presence. A few adults recognized that their visual triggers are numerous and frequent. For example, Irene said, "I see my mother everywhere, in all places, such as the mother holding her sleeping child on the subway, or the mother watching her daughter try on her prom dress.

These things make me very sad and lonely."

Movies and television shows can prompt the memory of a parent. Chuck explained connections to his father through two specific movies: *The Great Escape*, which they often watched together, and *Field of Dreams*, which ends with a father and son catching and throwing a baseball. Other adults described similar associations. Why would movies and television programs prompt recollections of the deceased parent? Common among these associations are depictions of families and parent-child relationships.

Sounds can also serve as associations. Alice spoke of being reminded of her father during certain songs at church. Cynthia described an item which many adults would consider priceless: "When I was a little girl, my parents and I use to make cassette tapes and would send them to my sister in Minneapolis...I got my dad and my mother's voice on there...that's a great thing to have." Basically all adults in this study grew up before video recording was common. Even if they were lucky to have home movies, there was usually no sound. A recording of the parent's voice or a parent's written word are different from one another, but both provide the opportunity for very personal connections.

Smells can also be powerful associations to the memory of a deceased parent. Zac admitted that he does not have a good sense of smell, yet his memory is prompted by a specific smell in a specific location: "Walking in the Saint James music hall...the smell. They put the same stuff on the floor that they did back then...I don't have a good sense of smell. I don't even notice some smells that people gag at." Chuck associates hunting with his father; therefore, "Just the smell of a shotgun..." can remind him of his father. Chad remembers his mom with a whiff of apple pie; Cynthia thinks of her mother when she smells a specific hand lotion; and Nancy thinks of her mother when she smells cardamom. She said, "It's more smells that trigger the memories for me, rather than sounds." As Nancy expressed, many adults recognize smells as one of their most common reminders of their parent.

Why are so many memories of deceased parents associated with the senses? Could it be that these primordial senses are a link to a deeper sense of the parent's presence? The senses become doorways to memories; the memories are connections to an absent parent.

People and Places

Associations may also be made between a deceased parent and another person or place. Individuals do not always remember why certain associations are created, but most of them have reasons. Chuck's association is between his father and John F. Kennedy. They died around the same time; they were in World War II; and they were individuals who Chuck admired in childhood. They both seemed to be heroes to Chuck.

Vi described a variety of associations that prompt memories of her father. Her associations serve as an illustration of the wide variety that a person may have. First of all, she recognized the state in which her father was born and raised, which is also the state where she was born: "Oregon—where daddy's from—holds a special place in my heart. If we go there or people mention that they are from there, my ears perk up. I think, 'That's Daddy. That's where he was from.'" She also thinks of him when she hears the name of the college where he last taught: "Daddy taught at St. James College. So if anything is mentioned about St. James College...Anything that is mentioned that involves him is like a magnet." Vi also recognized the father of a friend whom she associates with what her own father would have been like in his later years: "He's one who triggers in me. When I see him interacting with her. He's gentle. He's tender. He's quiet. He loves God. I kind of picture my dad that way. I see things like that—that trigger it."

Anniversaries and Holidays

Of all the different types of associations possible, anniversaries and holidays are the most common. Holidays are generally occasions in which family members come together. The void of a family member, especially a parent, can change the entire "feel" of the holiday. For many individuals, any holiday reminds them of their loss. Others have special circumstances that cause them to associate specific holidays with their parent.

Christmas and other major holidays are common occasions to remember a deceased parent. Mother's Day and Father's Day may not be considered major holidays by most people. For individuals that lost a parent, they can be as difficult, or more difficult, than major holidays. Rhonda acknowledged: "The hardest times for me was Mother's Day." Special circumstances also make the remembrance of a loss at certain holidays. For example, Alice's father died on Halloween: "The whole concept of Halloween turns me off, because it's not a day in which I want to joke around."

Death anniversaries are occasions in which an individual can revisit grief. On the other hand, a death anniversary can be a day to review the good memories of the deceased parent. These anniversaries are somewhat like private holidays. They mark the altering of life; they can be used to celebrate a life; they are shared among family members, whether they talk about it or not. In most cases, these anniversaries are experienced in a person's life without most friends and acquaintances knowing about it. Cynthia said, "For the first ten or fifteen years, I was very aware of death anniversaries, birthdays, Christmases. They were all triggers for me...I would feel so alone."

Adults, such as Jackie, understand anniversaries and holidays to be occasions to remember, include, or honor the memory of the deceased parent. "We had yellow roses at the funeral. And then, every year, at the anniversary of her death, I buy one, kind of as a memorial..." She also included the memory of her mother at her wedding with a floral wreath around the unity candle, which was later taken to the cemetery.

Sharing Memories With Others

An aspect of the experience is the sharing of memories. Sharing is defined: "To share is to give or receive a part of something; or to enjoy or assume something in common."[1] In two basic ways, adults describe their reasons for sharing memories: To *pass on* stories or objects of meaning *to* others; to *receive* stories or objects *from* others who hold memories of the deceased parent. It is a way in which the memories of the parent are recognized, strengthened, or passed from one to another. Sharing can help one recall past memories and various details of the memories. It can be a way of reliving memorable moments with the parent. It can also be a way to learn more about the deceased parent by hearing the memories of others.

Telling Memories

One way that individuals participate in sharing memories of their deceased parent is by describing their own memories, in order that others will know something about the parent. As Olivia recalled, "I speak of him often—just to remind people that he was here. Each time, I remember different things that I had forgotten over the years, and I always smile." Vi said, "It's amazing how quickly a person can be forgotten in history. It's such a short time-span. It is hard to balance between wanting to keep his memory alive and getting on with life and not dwelling on the loss."

The most common reason for sharing memories with others is to continue a family history and give children a knowledge of their deceased grandparent. Individuals feel that the sharing of memories with the next generation does not happen accidentally, but by a deliberate effort to share memories of their deceased parent.

Hearing Memories

Individuals, who have experienced the early death of a parent, would like to hear stories about their parent. Carl recalled, "Usually it was my uncles or my dad's friends that would bring up things like, 'Oh gee, he could really sing that song good;' or, 'We used to really have fun doing this or that.'" Carl expressed the importance of these moments as he could learn new things about his deceased father. Vi described a similar memory from childhood: "I always wanted to hear stories about my dad. Even now when I go and visit my grandparents or uncle...If there was ever anyone who said anything about my father, my ears would perk up, and I would want to hear stories about him." Cynthia also remembered such a moment with her cousin and aunt: "Her mom said, 'You know...when your mom and I were little girls'...she told us all kinds of really awesome stories..." She also said that storytelling should be practiced in passing on memories: "Storytelling and stuff—we all need to be doing that...There's got to be some way to keep this alive...through the generations." Although Cynthia does not have any children, she recognized the importance of sharing memories because she knew what it was like to be on the receiving end of sharing.

The sharing of memories is an example of individuals' efforts to reinforce the presence of their parent in their own memories and share them with others. For many, this began as a childhood desire to hear others' memories about their parent. Such sharing of memories is also important because it demonstrates, to the surviving children, that the parent is also present in the memory of others.

During interviews for this book, many adults displayed an enjoyment in sharing memories of their deceased parent. A number of them specifically stated that they enjoyed the experience of being interviewed more than they expected. For a number of adults, years pass between the occasions in which they talk about their loss and their memories of the deceased parent. Yet, adults interviewed for this book had an ability to share and recall memories that they had not pondered in a long time. In doing so, it was as if they were revisiting a familiar geographical location to which they had not been in some time.

What about those who lost a parent before an age at which memories were established? Adults, such as Amy and Billie, have relied solely on the memories that others have shared with them. Can one have a memory of a moment which they did not experience? Can one have a memory of a person in whose presence they do not remember being? Memory is: "The act or fact of retaining mental impressions." [2] These adults received their mental impressions of their parent through others. Yet it seems that their deceased parent is present in memory. Do they have exact pictures in their mind? If so, the pictures came from photos, videos, or oral descriptions.

Remembering the Parent in Unexpected Moments

A parent may come to remembrance in unexpected moments. Unexpected moments can occur through associations or times of sharing, as previously described; but they are different than previous examples in that there is an element of surprise and unpredictability. As Olivia explained, "It's funny how, just out of the blue, those feelings just pop up and hit you in the face. You never know when it will happen..." Laura also said, "Some of the things you don't think about, and then all of a sudden, you think, 'Where did that come from?'" Nancy shared a similar perspective: "All of a sudden, something might trigger something that comes completely out of nowhere. You think, 'Where did I get that? Oh yeah, it did happen.'"

Adults, interviewed for this book, noted that the interview prompted memories, feelings, and emotions which surprised them. Nancy was one such participant. She said, "It's funny how all of a sudden you can sense experiences or feel being there, where you have not thought about for thirty years." Others were surprised by their own recollections of their parents, which caused them to be teary-eyed during the interview.

Dreaming is another way in which memories may surface unexpectedly. They may become more infrequent from year to year, but can also occur longer than twenty years after the death. Irwin, fifty-five years past his father's death, said, "There are many times it passes through my mind. I used to dream of him, but I haven't dreamt of him in a long time, because our lives change." Vi recalled two specific dreams that she used to have as a child. Their frequency has lessened, but they continue to occur. She recalled,

> When I was a kid I used to have dreams. I still have them as an adult—very rarely—but I have had them. There are two different dreams. One dream is that he never actually died. He left. I don't know why he left, but basically he left and someday I run into him and I see him. I think, "That's my dad." The second dream is basically that he left, but he comes back; but my mom is remarried now. So life is not going to be the same as it was—ever. Life is never going to be the same. And basically, life isn't since he died. I wonder if the thought of him leaving is easier to deal with than the thought of him dying.

An unexpected encounter with feelings, as Chris recently experienced, can be prompted by an innocent discussion with one's own child:

> The other night, my son asked a question out of the blue. We had not been talking about my mom at all. His question was this: "Did your mommy kiss you and say, 'goodbye,' before she died?" I started bawling. I had gotten sad and cried before or during our talks, but this was different. I was literally sobbing.

Vi had an unexpected visual reminder in the appearance of a musician that looked like her father: "That brought back a memory. It was like, 'Oh, this could be my dad.'"

Summary

What does it mean to live with the loss of a parent that died in childhood or adolescence? It means that one's parent remains present in memory throughout life. Although many years have passed since the death of the parent—and although the death occurred in the growing-up years—the parent remains in memory. The memories are frozen in time, but many of them continue through time. They are frozen, but not necessarily forgotten. The parent's presence in memory is understood to both retain vividness in some aspects and fade in others. The parent's presence in memory is attached to various associations shared with others and found to surface at unexpected moments. There is an element of remembering that cannot be predicted, known, or controlled. Memories may come at unexpected moments and be caused by unexpected triggers.

Memories are of great importance to those who live with the early death of a parent. The memories serve as connections to the deceased parent; they provide a sense of the parent's presence. The individual has no possibility of experiencing new memories; therefore, they can only recall the ones that they already have. When memories lose vividness or simply dissipate with time, one may feel an added sense of loss.

Personal Insights

I have memories that are burned into my memory, and there are others that exist in pictures and super-eight films. In my mind, I remember my dad in a white tee-shirt and a green baseball hat, while laying brick and block; I remember him walking down a mountain in his florescent orange coat, attempting to scare a few deer towards me; I remember him in a flannel shirt, when I bagged my one and only animal: a wild turkey; I remember him in his Bermuda shorts and yellow roll-up hat, fishing on a pier in Ocean City; I remember him in a dirty, white tee-shirt and jeans, arriving home from work; I remember him in his blue turtleneck sweatshirt, on the last day he was alive in our house. The memories that exist only in memory mark the good and bad times, as they were the ones that were most often replayed in my mind.

The memories in pictures and film are priceless, but I have one complaint of my dad—something of which I am also guilty at times. It is very hard to see the person behind the camera. My dad did most of the filming; therefore, he is the least-filmed member of the family. In knowing how easy it is to remain the videographer, I make deliberate efforts to get in the picture so that my children will have more views of me. Something else that we have done for future generations is to put all pictures in to scrapbooks in which I have written captions that reveal details of family history.

There are associations, both in my possession and randomly seen in other places, which immediately make me think of my dad—both expected and unexpected. His old hunting and fishing equipment, bricklaying, light-blue Ford trucks, elk, Lymphoma, playing catch with my children, and many other things can prompt a memory of my dad.

When I was in my late elementary years, I went to a movie, *The Adventures of the Wilderness Family*,[3] with my dad. I had forgotten about that movie until a few months ago, when I purchased the *Wilderness Family* series for my family. The last time I watched that movie was in the late 1970s, next to my dad, in a theater near our home. I remembered that the movie represented my dad's love for the outdoors, but I had forgotten that the father in the movie, played by Robert Logan, looks much like my dad. I was pleasantly surprised by the experience, and I was pleased to tell my children that, besides our photos and eight-millimeter films, the man in the movie looks like my dad.

More than twenty years have passed since my dad died, yet I can identify recent, unexpected moments of remembering him. Recently, I walked by a construction site, where a mortar box was sitting, and I immediately thought of my dad, mixing mortar. It caught me by surprise. I am also surprised by dreams of him being alive. Such dreams have a number of years between them, but they still occur many years after his death.

A few months ago, I was given an audio tape of my grandfather, being interviewed and singing in Italian. Near the end of the recording, I heard my dad. I was stunned, because I had not heard his voice since the day before he died, and his voice sounded nothing like I remembered. The only recording of my dad's voice exists in a few seconds on that tape.

The most meaningful associations with my dad, and my wife's dad, are connected to our children. Daniela was named after my dad, David was named after Wendy's dad, and Jameson, named after our grandfathers, has a unique birth date. The date of my dad's death, December 5th, has come and gone many times since he died. Jameson was to be born in November, but God saw it fitting for him to be born late, on December 5th. His birth was in no way tainted by the previous recognition of that day. Instead, it is a double celebration of a grandfather's birth into eternal life and a grandchild's birth into this world.

For the Surviving Parent

- **Children need help in preserving memories.** Children will probably have memories of the deceased parent that the surviving parent does not have, but they will forever appreciate efforts to preserve memories—especially in their adult years. The surviving parent should consider becoming a scrapbook-maker or writer, if not already involved in such activities.

- **Children will value a gathering of others' memories.** Old friends, family members, or church members may hold memories of the deceased parent that children will want to know about in the future. The surviving parent can enrich their children's lives by compiling the memories of others. The children will appreciate this written history, especially in their adult years, when they want to know more about the testimony, upbringing, personality, and character of their parent.

- **Children want to have things that belonged to their parent.** This is true for children in the early years, but even more applicable to adults who experienced the early death of a parent. Many adults speak of the belongings of their deceased parent that were thrown out or given away. The surviving parent cannot keep everything, but for the sake of the children, they should keep as many items as possible.

- **Children would rather not leave the house in which they lived with their parent.** Financial strains and remarriage may prompt the family to move to a different home, but leaving the house in which their parent was a part of the family can be very difficult for a child. Like various belongings of the deceased parent, the child may feel that the house holds memories of the parent that are being abandoned.

- **Children should have their parent's death anniversary acknowledged.** Most people forget about death dates unless the date marks a great change in their own lives. In a number of families, the date is like the presence of an elephant in a room—everyone is aware of it, but they are not sure if they should talk about it. Families should not only talk about it, but they should use the day to share memories and address any reoccurring grief. The surviving parent may also want to ask friends and family members to mark the date on their calendars.

- **Children should be encouraged to share the unexpected moments of remembering.** A sight, smell, or dream will cause children to think about their deceased parent. At those moments they may want to keep it to themselves or share it with family members. The children should know that they are welcome to talk about those moments. Such openness is often communicated by the willingness of the surviving parent to share his or her own moments of remembering.

....

The LORD is near to the brokenhearted
and saves those who are crushed in spirit.
Psalms 34: 18

Chapter 8

Understanding and Defining Self

As described in previous chapters, the tour guide's departure was early in the journey. The tourist either knew the tour guide long enough to develop a dependence on his or her leading, or the tourist became aware of the tour guide later in the journey. In many cases, the teachings practiced along the journey became instilled within the tourist. As the tourist grows in travel experience, he or she often wonders about the resemblance of self to the absent tour guide. The tourist may actively search for those shared traits and practices, but he or she does not always know which of his or her traits and practices were passed on from the tour guide.

Another aspect of tourists' understanding of themselves is in how they were shaped by the journey without the tour guide. Although not always clearly understood, the tourists know that they were shaped by the tour guide. With much more clarity, the tourists believe that they were uniquely shaped by their journey without the tour guide. They were forced to become more strong, mature, and independent as their journey became a greater personal responsibility.

Being without the resources of the tour guide, the tourist often becomes a student of other tour guides, watching their traveling practices and interactions with tourists. In knowing that he or she will be a tour guide someday, the tourist prepares for tour guiding by observing others.

Also along the journey, the tourist encounters other tourists who have lost a tour guide or experienced another setback on their journey. Having been through the loss of a tour guide, the tourists understand loss and identify with others in loss.

The death of a parent in childhood or adolescence is an extraordinary event that separates two lives. It is an event that affects the ways in which life is lived, death is viewed, family is planned, and identity is formed. As one grows up with this loss, he or she arrives at different understandings of the impact of the loss on life. Somewhere on this journey, adults seem to ask themselves this question: "How has my loss affected who I am?"

One woman in her forties said, "It changed my life and my family life in so many ways that it's difficult to even know where to start." Another said, "In a nutshell, my father's illness and death were the defining moments of my life and made me into the person I am today, for better or worse." A deep understanding is evident in persons like Chad, a man in his forties who lost his mother when he was seventeen years old. He said, "It's certainly one of those life changing things that changes your entire life and how you view life, how you view relationships, how you view priorities."

Wondering How Life Would Have Been Different

What difference does the death of a parent make in defining a person? An Aspect of one's understanding involves the contemplation of life changes related to the loss. One uses understandings of the loss to examine the impacts on self. As Brooke said, "I believe I am a different person today than I would have been if my father had lived longer..." Irene described, "The loss sets patterns for the rest of your life...I find myself alternately pulling and pushing at my husband...Sometimes, I don't want to feel anything, and other times he couldn't tell me enough how he loves me."

Amidst understanding how self has been made different, one may also wonder how life would have been different. It is another way in which individuals attempt to make sense of the impact of their loss. On one side is understanding—at least an attempt to understand, what is different. On the other side is wondering what life might have been like if the parent had not died. As Irwin admitted, "There are times when I've thought back about how differently things may have been." Rhonda also said, "Sometimes I think…'What if she would have been around? How different would things be?'"

There are a variety of ways in which life would have been different if the parent had not died. Some ways are obvious; others are left to speculation. Amy lost her mother when she was only a few months old. She enjoyed being raised by her father and doing "guy" things with him. On the other hand, she suggested, "I might have turned out completely different. I might have been more feminine." Vi wondered if she would have made the same choice of college. She also said, "I've wondered what it would've been like to be a teenager growing up with a dad." Jackie said, "I've wondered how my wedding would've been different; relationships with in-laws would be different; having a baby would be different." Nancy became the main caretaker in her family. She said, "But, then you always wonder, what would the dynamics be…Because of the role I ended up taking, and because I have so many nurturing tendencies, would I have ended up taking that role if mom was alive?"

This wondering is not about obsessing about something that will never occur. As Nancy said, "Those are more 'what if' things that you just have to live without. You just don't know what those 'what-ifs' would be like, and that's what's so difficult." Vi said, "For me, it's been twenty-one years since he died. Sometimes it just seems unreal. It's hard to imagine what it would be like now. I have lived more of my life without him than I did with him. That is just a very strange feeling."

Although there are most likely no benefits to wondering, it is part of understanding. Possibly, it happens as individuals allows themselves to fantasize. It could simply be another way for an individual to understand how life has been altered forever; for others, it is a place that one does not need to visit any longer.

Whether one wonders or not, he or she knows that life is different from what it would have been. A definitive answer to "How?" is not possible. This is the only question that can be definitively answered in relation to this theme: "Is my life different than it would have been if my parent had not died?"

Understanding Specific Characteristics as Bi-products of the Loss

Those who live with this loss contemplate ways in which their lives have been changed; they sense that the loss helps define them as a person. Adults see specific characteristics in themselves as bi-products of the loss, which affects personality traits, social skills, fears, likes, and dislikes.

Strength

The brief example discussed in this section includes those descriptions in which adults reflected on how their loss made them a stronger person. Chad felt that his gained strength kept him motivated and able to keep priorities in order:

> The loss can become a strength. I certainly feel that way. I know it's what motivated me to be a good dad and a good husband. It is what I think has helped keep my priorities straight. It's what has shaped my life. It's always there.

Chad also connected his strong familial relationships to the strength he received out of his loss. Nancy recognized that her loss gave her strength which she may not have had otherwise: "As much as the loss was very monumental, it has probably given me a lot more positive strength than I would have thought I would have had." Rhonda described an understanding of strength that often comes from pain: "I think I've become a stronger person through the pain...because I can deal with a lot."

What is it about this loss that makes individuals feel stronger? For some, it is a bi-product of pain. This gained strength may also be a natural reaction to having one's innocent assumptions destroyed. As a person grows, he or she learns that living involves disappointments and losses, which can change the course of life. Children, who experience the death of a parent, learn this lesson earlier than most people. Their loss may "toughen them up" by teaching them that unexpected difficulties are possible realities. They may also be strengthened by enduring a loss that prepared them to face future losses; however, not everyone gains strength from the death of a parent.

Responsibility

When a parent dies, the family makeup is changed. This change often means a shift in responsibilities. Nancy, for example, became the primary homemaker and caretaker of her sister at the age of twelve:

> I became the chief cook and bottle washer. I was going from a typical childhood of being a kid. Before I was even a teenager, I had total responsibility of caring for a sister, who at that time was eight; being the woman of the house; and doing the cooking, cleaning, and meal preparation...I basically was running a household for a family of five. That removed me from a lot of the social activities of being a kid of twelve, going on thirteen. Then, I had all these other responsibilities that I had not necessarily prepared for, but had to assume.

As one might surmise, male adults spoke of taking on responsibilities that belonged to their fathers. Sam explained, "I stayed at home...My mother just really needed me...taking care of things around the house...fixing leaky faucets or shoveling the snow, or whatever..." Irwin said, "I felt that upon my father's demise, I had a responsibility." Kathy assumed some of her father's responsibilities in her mother's life: "She didn't drive at that time, so I was getting up early and driving her to work. I dropped out of GAA. I just knew that I had to do that. I had to do that for my mom."

Adults also admitted that added responsibility was not always easy. Rhonda said, "I do feel that there was a lot of responsibility put on me. Not that it was purposefully put there, but I took it upon myself…It was very hard." Although she felt that she made the right decision, Jackie wished that someone else would have taken on the responsibility of moving her out from living with her abusive father after her mother died.

With the addition of responsibilities, an individual may become a more responsible person. Individuals, such as Sam, felt that added responsibility translated into his becoming more responsible. He said, "I didn't want to do anything that would really make it harder for her…So that kind of always held me down a little bit—from really going out and doing crazy stuff." As Isabel said, "I think because I lost my mom and I didn't want to be such a burden to my father, I really focused on school. I tried to do the right things…" Becoming a more responsible person may also be the result of a conscious effort to avoid adding difficulty to the life of the surviving parent.

What is it about this loss that makes one more responsible? Having responsibilities and being responsible are expectations that commonly grow along with a child's level of understanding. When one experiences the death of a parent, this process is accelerated.

Maturity

Many individuals, who experience the early death of a parent, have a specific feeling of being more mature than their age warranted. Carl heard what might have been the most common phrase used by others when a son loses a father: "Now you and your brother have to be the men of the house." For children or adolescents, this expectation of maturity can be an added pressure to rid themselves of immaturity. This can be especially difficult for a child, since they already feel a life-altering loss and do not have the ability to force their own growth. Nevertheless, a number of individuals expect greater maturity out of themselves. For example, Irwin recalled this decision which he made as an adolescent: "At the time of his death I just realized, 'Now Irwin, you've got to be more of an adult'…I know that in my own mind I felt that I had to grow up fast and I did."

A gauge, often used in contemplating maturity, is seen in comparing and contrasting an individual to his or her peers—both by adults and the individual with the loss. Dan said, "I'd been told by a lot of people, at that age, that I was rather mature for a eight-nine-ten-year-old kid." Jackie expressed similar feelings, which stayed with her into adult life: "So, by the time I went through high school and got to college, I was just floored by other people my age and how immature they were, because, I'd been adult since I was thirteen." Carl also mentioned that he felt more mature when compared to his peers: "I do recall, growing up, that I felt like I was older than the kids around me. I wouldn't really say that then, but I was thinking it; even though in retrospect, I wasn't mature either. It was just a sense that I had."

It is possible that accelerated maturity can be a feeling that comes with enduring a loss which most do not have to endure. Chuck described the loss as a "badge" which many of his peers did not wear: "I went through something not everybody had to go through. So, I suppose in a way, it did accelerate my maturity..."

Emotions seem to be the main aspect of this sense of maturity. Mike specifically described his maturity as "emotional maturity." Laura said, "In some ways, I think you have to grow up... emotionally" Quinn said that emotional maturity came with experiencing so many emotions: "It seems you have to grow up so fast—you miss things—and you don't know how to handle them...It's hard to explain. It is because of the emotional things that you go through."

What is it about this loss that makes individuals feel more mature? Could it be that enduring a major loss simply makes a child feel a greater sense of maturity that is not normally felt? Could it be that a child feels an awakening—an opening of the eyes—to a world filled with tragedies and harsh realities? Could it be that a child really does "grow up" by encountering difficulties? Mike said, "It propelled me... as I went through the tough time...I grew in self-confidence." Could it be that a major loss simply makes a child feel that childhood is over and adulthood is beginning? As Irene said, "I felt so old, so young. I still do. I have to count back the years to remember that I am only twenty three. My life seems so long already." Life may seem "so long" to Irene because she, like many adults interviewed for this book, have had to prematurely begin adulthood.

Independence

When asked to clarify if they were describing accelerated maturity, adults often clarified by saying, "Independence." Independence may be a bi-product of maturity, but it was described as a distinct bi-product of the loss—a bi-product which adults specifically name.

For those who lose a parent at a young age, independence is a common characteristic. Its inception comes with the realization that with a parent gone, one has to be more responsible for oneself. As Irwin said, "I learned, in those high school years, that if I'm ever going to get ahead in this world, I've got to do it on my own." Rita recognized that her independence is connected to a realization that she could never depend on her mother's love again:

> I have learned that nothing replaces a mother, and I have to love myself. The biggest thing for me is believing in myself. I have learned this the hard way, and I probably wouldn't have learned it, hadn't it been for my circumstances. I can be extremely independent...

After her mother's death, Cynthia also realized that she would have to direct her own life:

> So, I think I learned to take care of myself at a pretty young age, in every way— emotionally...I am the only one, when the chips are down, that's going to take care of me... I've been taking care of myself, by myself, all these years... I think that my mother's leaving me, at a young age, forced me to be very independent...No matter how great things are, I feel like I'm running this life by myself.

Although persons may have a positive, nurturing relationship with their surviving parent after the death of a parent, they often feel, as Cynthia described: "I'm running this life by myself." Ian came to this realization at the age of fourteen: "When I was fourteen I remember realizing that as long as I'm alive I have someone to count on—me."

Independence is more than a phase following the loss; it is a lifelong personal characteristic. It is also a survival mechanism and a way of life. "Fiercely independent" was a phrase that both Nancy and Blythe used to describe themselves as a result of their loss. Similar to the descriptions of others, Nancy explained her independence as a learned lesson, received through needing to figure things out for herself:

> Some of the foundations that you face, you have to figure out yourself—where other people have the instruction guide coming from an oral presentation. For me, it was basically trying to figure it out on my own. You can either, look at your loss, and become a depressed kid, and act out the opposite way, or you channel it, and figure out, and learn from it. That's probably what shaped me. It made me more independent. It made me a lot stronger. It's given me the impetus to have talents and skills in areas that I probably would have never developed, because there's always somebody who does that for you. It's really made me who I am today.

Nancy's gained independence shaped her talents, skills, and whole person. Today, she is a leader in a career position that is mostly held by men.

As seen in Nancy's description, this feeling of independence can be something that pushes a person to achieve. Mike said, "It kind of released me to stand up a little bit more on my own. I kind of excelled a little bit from it…It pushed me to be much more independent…" Not only did Jackie feel confidence in independence, but she is also very proud that she has accomplished much on her own. Chuckling, she recalled this moment with a coworker:

I said to one of my coworkers, "My step-mom just sent me ten dollars in the mail today. I've never had that before." And she said, "Oh, I always pictured you as daddy's spoiled little girl." And I thought, "That couldn't be farther from the truth....I put myself through college and I haven't had a parent for fifteen years, thank you."

What is it about this loss that makes one more independent? This characteristic is the result of learning that surviving children must do more for themselves. To a greater extent than most children, they are forced to take responsibility for their own life. Although independence is created out of a childhood loss, in adulthood this characteristic continues shaping life and affecting career choices and other decisions. Adults label this characteristic in different ways—fierce independence, automatic dependency, self-sufficiency—and they also recognize that it is a life-long characteristic resulted from their loss. However, not all persons, touched by this loss, recognize independence as a bi-product of their loss.

What does it mean to live with this loss? It means that as individuals grow in understanding their loss, they contemplate the ways in which they have been changed. This includes those personal characteristics that were formed by their loss and continue into adulthood. As the loss signaled the ending of childhood and the beginning of adulthood, it also signaled the accelerated growth of adult-like characteristics.

Attempting to Discover the Influence of the Parent

Years after the death of a parent, one may seek answers to such questions: "What did my parent teach me?" "What examples did he live?" "What did I get from her?" The process of discovery may be a deliberate attempt to understand. It may also be a chance encounter.

Recognizing that Some Lessons Are Untaught, Unlearned, and Unfinished

When life is shortened for a parent, a child misses lessons that the parent would have taught. Laura called this loss, "unlearned lessons." Zac recognized this loss as "unfinished" lessons: "Most of what his loss meant to me, I think, is perhaps that his lessons were unfinished; but that doesn't help me emotionally deal with it, because I don't know how he would finish them or if there would be anything else." Zac later linked a few of his current frustrations to the unfinished lessons of his father. As seen in the previous quote, Zac acknowledged that his father may not have finished or added to the lessons that he taught. Nevertheless, he speculated that his father would have finished his lessons:

> He was very much a perfectionist—always wanting a better job... Things always had to be right. He was the type of person who would say, "Nothing is worth doing if you can't do it well," which isn't true... There are some things you don't need to do perfectly, but he wasn't that way. When you are that way.....success isn't really success, it's just the way things should be.....and you can only fail. That's very much how I felt. Maybe he would have expanded on those lessons. He didn't really teach those lessons to me directly. He didn't sit down and say those things to me, but I knew how he was. I knew how he wanted things. So it seems like my whole life, instead of trying to succeed, I've been running from failure. I could shoot myself in the foot because of that. At this point in my life, I do blame my dad. He died when I was eleven. There was a lot more that he could have said or taught, and I don't know how things might have gone from there.

Zac later admitted that he came to such conclusions in the past few years. He is now thirty-two, not remembering his father with the same degree of fondness that he felt in the past. As various dreams have not come to fruition in his life, he looks to the unfinished, unedited, or unchanged lessons of his father, which would have made him less "bound" by perfectionism.

What is the significance of untaught, unlearned, and unfinished lessons in the discovery of the deceased parent? The answer is found in the fact that certain lessons will never be taught or completed by the deceased parent. There are parent-to-child contributions, which can only be classified as what-might-have-been or what-could-have-been.

One of those secondary losses felt by a person, who experienced the early death of a parent, is a lost opportunity to receive something valuable from a person, who will never return. With a shortened opportunity to receive lessons from a parent, the child is left to contemplate what he or she received. Vi said, "You are growing up and you are who you are because of them, but you can't remember why."

Idealizing the Parent

The idealization of a deceased parent may become part of a person's thought process. As one wants to remember and assume the best qualities of the parent, he or she may allow any negative qualities to be ignored and positive qualities to be exaggerated. As Zac said, "I guess part of the other thing is, for a lot of years, I thought of him as being the perfect father." Zoe's idealization served as a standard to measure all men against: "I drifted emotionally through relationships with the opposite sex. Part of the reason was that I could never find a man who I thought was as good as my father." Alice admitted idealizing her father, but she also recognized that it has helped her deal with the loss:

> I think—or maybe I've created this hope—that my dad would have kept our family a little more closely knit. I have studied a lot of psychology and have analyzed my feelings. I think I have idealized my father—focused more on the good memories than bad ones, and I tend to think he would fix anything bad that happens, if he was just still here. In reality, I know that isn't true, but it's a way for me to deal with it.

Zac's idealization of his father also involved the creation of personal expectations that Zac did not meet:

> I always thought I would emulate my dad. When I was around twenty-six, it really hit me hard…realizing where

my dad was at that point and where I expected to be. And at twenty-six, I expected that I would have had my doctorate, and I would be teaching college music...It's too late, and it's frustrating.

In Zac's creation and loss of the expectation he described, he seemed to feel that he was failing his father by not being like him. As a person sets up an idealization of a parent, he or she may either be motivated to attain to the idealization or be overwhelmed by the impossibility of achieving such perfection.

The relationship between the child and the deceased parent may be likened to a magnetic force. Memory of the deceased parent pulls the child to be like him or her. A child may also feel repelled or pushed away to be unlike the deceased parent. In both cases, the parent is a force in shaping the life of the child.

Attempting to Understand Self in Light of Parent's Influence

Although the time, which adults had with their parent, ended prematurely, adults recognized that their parent taught them something. Irwin didn't describe specific details, but he displayed a confidence in knowing that his father taught him important lessons: "I still feel that there were some ethics that I was taught before he died—that were instilled in me." Jackie saw a natural progression in living what her mother taught her: "She started shaping my choices for the future when she was living. After her death, I just continued that stuff."

An aspect of discovering oneself, in relation to the deceased parent, involves deciding the ways in which self has been impacted by that parent. The question answered is this: "What of me is because of them?" This is not always about individuals who want to find themselves. It is about understanding what childhood impacts, originating from the deceased parent, have carried into one's values, habits, and whole being.

It seems that living with this loss, for many, means that persons are more responsible to define themselves rather than be shaped by a parent. This does not discount the involvement of the surviving parent. In many cases, the surviving parent continues to contribute to the shaping of the child. Cynthia said, "Who I am is who I am without my mother." She also said, "I know who I am." One may then wonder, "Of all the things that define and identify me, which ones are from my deceased parent?"

Although not all individuals who live with this loss are able to identify who they are as a result of their parent, many exhibit a confidence in knowing that the deceased parent had an impact. Irene said, "I know I'm a different person than I ever would have been if she hadn't died. That is the impact, plain and simple." Although she does not remember the details of her upbringing, Vi is confident that her father was instrumental in shaping who she is: "I just feel that he did a good job with instilling those values in me, even though I don't remember specific things."

Being Like the Deceased Parent

Being like the deceased parent may be a deliberate endeavor by those who experienced the early death of a parent. Cynthia said, "I'm on a quest. Trying to get my mother's traits back so that I can have them in my life." Nancy tried to replicate her mother's traits in the past, but she realized that she was free to be herself: "Those kinds of things I saw from her of what I thought an ideal wife and mother was—I tried to replicate for years. I was living some type of fantasy that wasn't real." Oscar also tried to reproduce his learned style of manhood. Like Nancy, he realized his approach was futile: "Years back, I used to try to be more aggressive, because that was my perception of manhood...Well, I couldn't be that person and I knew I couldn't. After a number of years, I just said, 'I can't pull this off. It's not me.'" Adults often spoke of an effort to define themselves.

Character and personality traits, of deceased parents, serve as specific ways in which their children may try to be like them. Cynthia recognized traits of her mother, such as compassion and loyalty. She said, "She was very sympathetic. I know I have that part. ...my friendships are like the kind my mother had...the people that I actually count on are actually few, and I know my mother had friendships like that too." Olivia said that she is like her father in a lot of ways, particularly in being compassionate: "My Father was a very quiet, compassionate man. I feel, now that I am grown, that I am like him in a lot of ways."

Who am I because of my parent? Most individuals with this loss will never have a complete answer to this question. Others feel that they have an accurate understanding of their parent's impact. As one seeks to answer the question, an examination of likeness can be a starting point. In many cases, adults have striven to adopt their parent's practices in their life. Chad said that he wanted to model everything about his mother: "She was definitely my idol growing up... I just wanted to be like her. I admired her for her faith, for her caring qualities. She always cared about other people. She took people into her house that were in crises—things like that."

Being Unlike the Deceased Parent

In discovering the deceased parent, adults also contemplate the differences between themselves and the deceased. Amy speculated that she must be unlike her mother, since she was raised by her father:

Well, I've thought sometimes that I am perhaps a little bit masculine because of the association with my dad... I've been more physically active in sports and things. I play golf, tennis, swimming, and all those things, so I don't know if that is an influence from my father, or if that is my makeup. I've been interested in baseball and football because that's what I heard on the radio... I was with my dad and he took me to ball games and hockey. He was a sports person, and I was more of a boy to him.

Mike remembered a difference between he and his mother. The "artsy" things that he enjoyed were things that she viewed as silly: "She was real critical and condescending if I didn't do certain things. A lot of things that I did, she classified as silly...I loved that kind of stuff—painting, sketching..." Mike later explained that when his mother died, he was free to pursue the things he liked.

Adults also strive to be different from their deceased parent. Zac shared this explanation:

Do you ever watch Frazier? There was a show the other night—when he got the award for a lifetime achievement. He went back to his mentor and his mentor said, "Why did you become a psychiatrist?" That kind of hit a note with me, in a way. It was to distance himself from what his father was. I think I do some of that myself.

A few individuals reflected on their parent's communication of love as something that motivated them to be different. Irwin decided that he would communicate love to family members in ways which were deliberate and verbal: "I never heard my father utter those words, so I made a deliberate stance in my life, that I'm not going to leave this world without telling people that I love them." The expression of love was the same issue that Quinn recalled from his father's life:

My father didn't know how to love more than one person. That was difficult....I went home one time when I was in the military. I went home and I wanted to ask something of my mother. I said, "Mom, why didn't dad love me?" She said, "Well." I said, "Maybe I don't wanna know." That told me that what I was feeling was right. I said, "I don't wanna know. I know now that he didn't." She just said that he had trouble loving more than one person at a time.

Seen in Quinn's descriptions throughout his interview, was a deliberate effort to live much differently than what he saw modeled in the life of his father. He explained that he has close, loving relationships with his children and grandchildren.

Being Worthy of the Parent's Pride

In deciding the impact of a deceased parent on one's identity, a number of individuals desire to become a person worthy of their parent's pride. As Olivia expressed, "I hope that I have become someone he would be proud of." Vi said, "There is a part of me that still wants to do what's right to please my daddy."

Having a sense of making the parent proud seems to be the impetus for individuals to live responsibly. Dan explained his feelings:

> I think the vision of my mother, the presence of my mother not being there—but being there—kept me out of trouble. From the standpoint of, "If I did that, what would mom think?" At that time I would think, "Is she able to see what I'm doing? Is she looking down on me from heaven? I want her to be proud of me as a son."

Isabel described a similar desire. She also explained that she thinks about her mother's guidance when she has a big decision to make:

> Sometimes I'll think, "What would my mom want me to do," in a situation. Like, career wise, when I was going to college, and things like that. "Would she be proud of me? Am I doing what she had always dreamed for me?" I do what I think would make her proud.

At times, adults are also concerned about the approval that their parent would have for their spouse. In reference to her husband, Jackie said, "Well, getting married, as far as my mom goes…I knew that she would just love the man I married. She would just totally approve of him." Cynthia expressed similar sentiment in reference to her boyfriend: "My mother would love him because he love's me."

It seems that most individuals want to believe that the deceased parent would be proud. Although the parent is gone, many feel the responsibility to live in a way that would make them proud. Zoe expressed it in a unique way: "I try to live my life in a way that honors my parents…" More than seeking a sense of the deceased parent's pride, individuals may simply feel the responsibility to honor the deceased parent in their behavior and choices.

Understanding oneself involves drawing connections between the deceased parent and one's own characteristics and values. What did that parent deliberately teach? What did that parent model? In what ways has life been impacted by the parent? What about me is

When God Became ApParent

because of my parent? Uncovering answers to these questions is part of the discovery. Although it is not always a deliberate endeavor, discovery of the deceased parent's influence on self is a way of understanding one's own identity.

In many different ways, the early death of a parent involves evaluation and identification. Chad said that the loss forces one to seek understanding, especially in reference to one's identity. He said, "It just forces you, I think, to think about that whole process of who you are. You understand how they've shaped your life so much clearer than if they hadn't passed on." Chad indicated that without the loss, one would not seek to understand the parent's impact with the same urgency with which the loss forces one to seek.

Defining Aspects of Identity by Observing Others

When a primary parent, teacher, and role model is gone from one's life, many lessons must be learned from other sources. As Blythe said, "...I have become a great observer." This section is about the sources, other than parents, which adults recognize as their educators of life. From individual people, adults gain knowledge and experience, which help them in defining themselves and growing.

As previously mentioned, Amy was raised by her father and felt that she missed out on learning about managing a household and making a hospitable home. She spoke with great appreciation about the neighbors from whom she learned when she was a newlywed: "But I learned from others...That was an area where they were so open to us and friendly and loving. They took us into their hearts. It was through them that I learned so many things."

Oscar spoke much about learning through observation. He did it as an adolescent, a college student, and a parent. He recalled this from his high-school years: "Sometimes I'd be invited to dinner. There would be several kids, and the father and mother eating. I'd be at the same table, and there would be conversation going around... I would think, 'This is wonderful.'" Later in life, when married and embarking on parenthood, Oscar observed other parents in his neighborhood:

Fortunately for us, when we got married and we moved back

here, we ended up in a neighborhood which had a lot of couples with kids. I think I watched and observed. I really got involved with these couples in softball and parties. Of course, they had kids, so all these kids would get together. Of course, when there were that many men around with their young kids, I saw how they reacted to what their kids were doing or saying...I picked up a lot of good stuff there. I think I had to do that.

Amidst these periods in life, Oscar was regularly inquisitive and eager to learn:

> I would rely on information from books, TV, or friends—just even in conversations. I don't know anything specific, but I do know I would ask questions like, "What did you do?" I'd try to find out what their reaction was to situations.

As Oscar relied on his observations to plan his individual roles as husband and father, he noticed that the time he spent with families, in adolescence, came back to him as examples to emulate: "I could only relate to other kids' families. They were from large families too. If somebody were to say, 'What would you do in this or that situation?' I think my thoughts would go back to there...Those were the images in my mind."

Observing came down to one basic thing for Oscar: "Hopefully, what I did along that line in pursuing my fatherhood...I was trying to pick up the better things of what a father should be, rather than pick up the bad things." Oscar's practice of observation serves as an illustration of the learning process which one may experience as he or she seeks to learn the lessons which may have originated from the parent if he or she had not died. Ian described a similar outlook:

> Since I don't have a mother or father to help me figure out life, I need to choose role models and pay close attention to what they have to say. The reason I need to pay close attention to my role models is that I substitute them for parents. Don't most people in tough situations ask themselves "What would mom or dad do in this situation?"

An aspect of observation is the opportunity to choose one's own desired practices. An individual may choose from a number of possibilities for living one's life. At the same time, people may make many choices based on their parents' direction. When one loses a parent, he or she enters a process that is like building a puzzle, collecting pieces from different puzzle boxes. The pieces will fit together well enough, even though the different puzzle boxes belong to other people. Sometimes people deliberately offer a piece to the one making a puzzle; at other times, the one making a puzzle forms replicas of the pieces that they like. Either way, the puzzle maker borrows from others.

Identifying with Others Who Experience Loss

An understanding, a connection, a sense—each is a different way in which adults describe the bond felt for another who has experienced loss—especially the loss of a parent in childhood or adolescence. Chad said, "I know what you felt like. You know what I felt like. It's one of those experiences that you don't want anyone else to go through, but having gone through it, you definitely feel the pain." As Isabel grew up, she felt that she was the only one who experienced the pain of losing a parent. This changed as she grew up:

> I felt like I was the only one who had ever experienced this—like I was the only eight-year-old who had lost their mother. As I get older, I notice, "Wow, this has happened to so many different people." I think, definitely, that I feel a connection when somebody says that they lost their mother or father when they were younger...Sometimes the whole effect of it is hard to put into words... because I don't really have to say too much about it

Chuck referred to his loss as a "badge" in his childhood and adolescent years. When asked to say more about his use of the term, Chuck said:

> I've never been in the military, but I respect people who

have been. They've been there and done that. I've kind of been through the same thing. I kind of know what it's like to go through. You know other people who have gone through that. We can relate and understand that unwritten or nonverbal...I kind of know what they've gone through, and they know what I've gone through.

Those who experience the death of a parent in childhood or adolescence do not usually meet many other individuals who have experienced the same loss. Many of them mature while living with a sense of aloneness in their loss. In adulthood, when the number of acquaintances and friends increase, they discover that others share the loss; others wear "the badge." In turn, they identify with others who have similar understandings.

Having been through a major loss, they can feel especially empathetic towards others with a loss. For a number of adults, the connection with others in loss is especially felt towards children. Others said that they feel a connection to anyone who experiences the death of a loved one. One man described it as "an unspoken understanding." Nancy alluded to the fact that she feels a stronger connection to someone who can be empathetic, as a result of their loss, rather than sympathetic.

Without distinguishing between the types of losses which others experience, Sam said, "I guess, in a way, it has made me more aware of the pain that people are feeling." Chris expressed a similar sentiment: "I have always been very empathetic and compassionate, rooting for the underdog. I have no problem feeling someone else's pain." For many individuals, empathy may be felt in relation to others with any type of loss.

Adults with this loss often find that their empathy is specifically felt towards children who have lost a parent. Rhonda described a situation in which the loss experienced by two children brought her to tears, because she empathized with their loss: "We just had a family in our church who has two little kids, I think they're around two and four years old. Those kids just lost both of their parents. I just heard about it, and I sobbed. I cried, because I understand." Rhonda, who has an adult understanding of the loss, was deeply saddened for the two children, who were too young to understand the life-long magnitude of their loss. Quinn also conveyed a definite understanding for children who have experienced loss:

> I think my loss has made me more sensitive to kids' loss... Parents, I mean adults, can deal with it. We can rationalize it in our mind. We can think about it. We can work it through. Kids know, "Hey, they're gone." If I'm gonna go one direction, it's gonna be to the kids. Even in mediation of family squabbles, I tell the adults, "It's not about you. This is about this kid, so get off of it." I think it makes you more sensitive too, to single moms trying to do the best they can do.

It may seem ironic that adults, who felt an absence in their child-hood, often become a strong presence in the lives of others with an absence. For a number of people, it seems to be a natural outgrowth of their loss. Amy is such a person. She has no memories of her mother, yet in living with her loss, she became a mother to a number of people, beyond her own children: "There were certainly a number of kids that I have been a mother to... they were always welcome here and it was a joy to have those kids around... I think that is very ironic."

Adults, who live with the absence of a parent, understand the importance of a parent's presence in the life of a child. As they become such a presence in the life of a child, they know that they are meeting a great need, which the child may not yet understand or appreciate. Nancy described an occasion in which she and others mothered a girl who lost her mother. She also described her ongoing effort to reach out to others:

> I don't care who's parent dies within my one-hundred and twenty employees. If it's physically within a distance to get there, I'm there. I have many adult friends, who at this time of life, still feel uncomfortable giving a word of condolence, or going to a visitation or a wake or a funeral. They just don't understand the *presence* of a

supportive person.....how important that is.

Within Nancy's description was an emphasis on the "presence of a supportive person." Once again, the importance of presence was emphasized. Kim said this about her loss and her ability to be a presence: "The person I became as a result of her death was a person who could *be there* for people who were experiencing hard times."

For many individuals, the loss has shaped them into a person who will reach out to others who experience loss. Ian formed a mission out of his loss: "Someday, God willing, I hope to be able to teach young men to be successful...I remember being exploited because I didn't have an older person to guide me. So, here I am, at twenty-nine years old, with a mission, a reason to be alive..." For Ian, loss makes more sense when it is used to positively affect the lives of others.

According to adults, one of the personal characteristics developed through the loss, is knowing how to respond to people who experience loss. As Alice explained, understanding others in loss involves knowing what words and actions should be avoided: "I have a great compassion for those who lose loved ones, and also a sense of what not to say at visitations and funerals." After the death of her mother, Nancy learned how to support others in very practical ways:

> Experiencing death within my family, at an early age, taught me how to support others in death... being able to come to the funeral...learning about bringing food to help. Learning about having people show up at the visitation when they didn't say anything but "Hi." That was a really important lesson that I learned—sensitivity to how you support people in their time of loss.

What was Nancy talking about? Is there something healing in funeral food or the expression, "Hi?' Not necessarily. What Nancy is talking about is being a presence—even when one does not know what to say. Most grieving people do not need to hear words as much as they need presence. Nancy also said that the wrong way to respond to someone is "absence of presence."

People often find themselves in contact with others who have experienced loss. A common inner struggle seems to be, "What should I say?" This question may lead to a paralyzing fear that causes one to avoid another person in loss. Usually, there are no "right" things to say which will fix the situation. As Vi said, "You just know how it hurts and feels. You don't know what to say. I don't know what to say still. You just feel awkward to say anything, because there's nothing to say. There's nothing you can say to make it better and take away the pain and loss." Kathy said this:

> When someone has lost a loved one, you need to be sensitive to what you say, and allow that person to talk... as long as I'm sensitive to the other person...All I have to say is, "How are you doing?" I don't have to worry about what I'm saying, as long as I'm sensitive.

Based on lessons learned during the early years of the loss, adults understand how to approach others with sensitivity. Most people have difficulty in finding words to express to one who has endured a loss. Yet, those who have experienced a loss often learn both what to say and what not to say. They learn, from experience, that besides being healing, words can be empty or hurting. What people may offer, as words of condolences, are not always perceived in the same manner. Kathy expressed her feelings related to this aspect of living with the loss:

> I know that when my dad died, people said, especially to my mother, "Let us know if there's anything you need. Let us know if there's anything I can do for you." Mother had that help immediately. Then, you're left alone... People, when they are saying, "Let me know if I can help you," they mean right now. They are not saying, "I'm going to help you for the rest of your life." They're saying, "If there is something you need right now, I'll do it for you." What they aren't saying is that they are going back into their families, to recover their life—to live the life that they have been living. They don't realize that your pain is going to endure past that week, past that month. It doesn't

end in a week. It doesn't end in a month.

Rhonda shared the same sentiment about what people mean when they give certain responses:

> You always have the crowd who say, "Oh, call me any time. I'll do whatever I can do for you…and blah, blah, blah, blah, blah." The ones who really meant a lot were those who would stay to be your friends. They didn't dwell on the subject. They didn't show all this creative sympathy. They were just *there* and said, "What do you want to do today?"

As adults talk about the early death of their parent, it is obvious that their loss, and others' responses, shaped them into a person who is sensitive to others in loss. Many learned important lessons on how to, and how not to, respond to others who experience a loss. A number of people with this loss, in turn, use their learned sensitivity to be there for others, which is discussed further in another chapter.

Summary

What does it mean to live with the death of a parent that occurred in childhood or adolescence? It means that individuals understand themselves in relation to the loss and the ways in which it has shaped them. In an effort to understand and define oneself, one will wonder, "How has my parent's death affected me? In what specific ways has the loss made me into who I am rather than who I would have been? What about me is from my deceased parent? What life lessons, which I did not learn from my parent, can I learn from observing the lives of others? In what ways has my loss affected how I relate to others in loss?" As persons endeavor to answer these questions, they grow in their understanding of themselves and the impact of their loss. They are individuals defined by their loss in many ways.

Personal Reflection

Was my dad's death a detour from my course of life? In seeing life through the perspective of God's will, I have to answer, "No," yet life following a tragedy often seems like a detour from the ideal. If my dad had not died, what aspects of God's will would not have been accomplished in my life? Stephen Curtis Chapman sang, "God is God and I am not. I can only see a part of the picture He's painting."[1] How exciting to know that there is a bigger plan beyond what we can see! How exciting to know that I can put my life in the hands of one who directs it better than I could on my own!

My dad was a three-year-old Christian when he died. What would his walk with the God look like today? I have been profoundly impacted by his death. How would I be different from who I have become? My dad worked in a profession unlike mine. Would I have felt the freedom to choose? God used my loss to shape me into me. Without the loss, what would I have been like?

Many years ago, I thought about the "what ifs" that may have prevented my dad's death. My dad died of a disease from which many people currently survive. What if today's medical discoveries existed then? My dad discovered lumps around his waist that led to his diagnosis. What if he would have noticed them sooner?

I remember watching the movie, *Back to the Future*,[2] when I was in high school. I watched the main character travel back in time in a sports car, and I thought, "What if time travel was possible? I could go into the past and make sure that my dad's disease was treated sooner." The same thinking could be used with the death of my wife's father: What if someone could have prevented Wendy's dad from getting in the car on the day of the accident? What if someone could have directed the driver to take a different route to the softball game? What if someone could have caused the car to be a few seconds early or late?"

The "what-if" line of thinking treats the tragedy as an event that could have been prevented, but the truth is: God allowed those things to happen, and we can trust that He knows what He is doing. Did God give my dad Lymphoma? Did God direct a car to swerve into oncoming traffic and hit the car in which Wendy's dad was a passenger? I don't believe so. Does God allow specific things to happen, in order that His purpose is accomplished? Yes. Do events also occur in our sinful world without divine direction, followed by God's work of making good out of bad? I assume so, but my human mind cannot totally understand the workings of an all-knowing, all-powerful, eternal God. What really matters is that we have faith in Him, no matter what comes our way.

H. Norman Wright wrote,

> Every loss is important. It is part of life and cannot be avoided. Losses are necessary! You grow by losing and then accepting the loss. Change occurs through loss. Growth occurs through loss. Life takes on a deeper and richer meaning because of losses. The better you handle them, the healthier you will be and the more you will grow. No one said that loss was fair, but it is part of life.[3]

He also wrote, "Loss produces maturity. There are character qualities such as patience, endurance, humility, long-suffering, gratitude, and self-control that can develop through our losses."[4]

The personal bi-products of my loss are as those described by the individuals interviewed for this book: strength, responsibility, maturity, and independence. I was strengthened by God, and I knew that He was bringing me through something that would be unbearable without Him; I felt more mature as I endured pain that most children did not bear; I acted responsibly, out of respect for God and my dad. Descriptions of the fourth bi-product, independence, was a new realization for me. I had always attributed my independence to being an only child; therefore, I did not foresee this as a common trait among those who experienced the early death of a parent.

My loss caused me to be more sensitive to loss and those touched by it. This is obvious in the effect that certain dramas have on me. Movies, shows, stories, or real-life accounts can move me to tears—especially if they involve a parent and child. I am moved by: the scene in the movie, *Father of the Bride*,[5] in which Steve Martin's character and his daughter are having their last conversation before her marriage; the scene in the movie,

Field of Dreams,[6] when Kevin Costner's character says, "Hey dad, you wanna catch?;" the scene in the movie, *Hope Floats,*[7] when a little girl begs her father not to leave their family; the video clip of Derek Redmond, in the 1992 summer Olympics,[8] when he pulled a hamstring during the 400-meter semifinals and was helped around the track by his father. As I identify with those who have experienced the loss of a loved one—especially the early death of a parent—I pray that God will use this book to help them in their loss.

For the Surviving Parent

- **Children may appreciate recognition of how their loss has positively impacted them.** Such a conversation should not happen for a number of years. Nevertheless, a child, teenager, or adult would appreciate these positive observations.
- **Children will appreciate knowing about the ways in which they are like their parent.** Adults describe this desire as something that grows in adulthood, many years after the death. The surviving parent can alleviate this search by communicating such observations throughout the child's life. Most children would be excited to know that they are like their deceased parent, who is often viewed as a hero.
- **Children will benefit from knowing about the ways in which they were impacted by their parent.** Similar to the previous point, individuals may want to know, especially in adulthood, how they were shaped by the deceased parent. Although obvious answers may not exist, a child may wonder, "What about me or my family is because of my parent's efforts?"
- **Children enjoy knowing that their parent would have been proud.** A number of individuals demonstrate a desire to live in such a way that their deceased parent would be proud. The surviving parent can help their children to be satisfied in this quest by saying, "Your father/mother would be so proud." A statement such as this will be very meaningful, especially in times of achievement.
- **Children will probably identify with situations of loss and change.** It should not be surprising if children develop a strong

sensitivity to the losses of others. Movies, books, and real-life stories may be occasions for children to become teary- eyed when they identify with another's loss. Similar feelings may surface in moments when family members are reunited—especially parent and child. The surviving parent should not be afraid to ask their children what they are feeling or thinking about.

- **Children should be encouraged to use what they have experienced to help others.** The surviving parent can give their children a vision of helping others in the future, which may be one of God's reasons for their loss. A statement such as, "Maybe God will use you to help others who experience the loss of a loved one," may be the catalyst for living out a God-ordained purpose.

....

"For I know the plans that I have for you," declares the LORD,
"plans for welfare and not for calamity
to give you a future and a hope."
Jeremiah 29:11

Chapter 9

Influence of Loss
in Family Living

As a tourist, without a tour guide, grows into an experienced traveler, he or she will be faced with the decision of becoming a tour guide. One may choose to continue traveling at his or her own pace without having the responsibility of guiding others. On the other hand, many choose to become a tour guide—to become responsible for the growth and safety of inexperienced tourists. Knowing what it feels like to lose a tour guide, and knowing that the journey is unpredictable, the traveler thinks about the possibility of being forced to abandon the tourists. These thoughts may prevent or delay travelers from deciding to be tour guides.

Because the traveler, who becomes a tour guide, knows that an unexpected departure is possible, he or she travels the journey with deliberate steps and frequent communication with the tourists. In preparation for a possible, unexpected departure, the tour guide lays markers along the way, which will serve as reminders of the tour guide's presence. The tour guide who lost his or her own guide on an earlier leg of the journey leads very deliberately. He or she feels that there are no distractions important enough to veer away from leading tourists along the journey.

Intentional Family Planning

This aspect of the loss reflects a sharp awareness and intentionality about family—whether to start a family and how to be a family. Adults, who experienced the death of a parent in childhood or adolescence, have developed specific ideas about what a family is and what a parent should be. They have definite plans for their own roles as parents and spouses. They usually live intentional lives.

Many adults, such as Quincey, conveyed an inner desire to have their own family. She said,

> After my mom died, I wanted a family of my own. I wanted something to fill the void...I got married when I was twenty-one and had my daughter at twenty-two. I had my priorities completely rearranged because of Mom's death. I know nothing is certain; never hold back.

Others, such as Cynthia, said that their loss encouraged them to avoid parenthood. Cynthia made a definite decision to have no children:

> I didn't want to leave any kids behind and have them go through what I went through...I went and had the surgery, so I actually can't have children...I don't know when it all clicked in my mind—probably about high school, when I had a family planning class...

Cynthia understood the pain of losing a parent. She did not want to risk being responsible for allowing another child to endure the same loss.

Carl, in his forties and not married, said that his loss fostered in him a fear of abandonment. He said that opening himself up to someone means risking the future loss of that relationship. For him, it is safer to simply control his own life as a single man. In contrast, Mike said that he developed a desire to "regain a sense of family." He expressed, "After my mom passed away...that was the end of my family as I knew it. I started looking to get married...I was waiting to have my own home...I was waiting to have that family unit again."

Among the adults interviewed for this book were two pairs of siblings. One pair consisted of twin males; the other was a female and male, less than two years apart in age. Especially in related to their loss's impact on family planning, these siblings approached their loss in very different ways. Although different, their experiences described the same theme. In each pair, one sibling chose to avoid creating a family while the other deliberately created family. In each pair was a single person, without children, and a married person, with three children of their own. The singles admitted that they think about the possibility of starting their own families, but they have become very used to single-living. The singles also admitted that their response to loss was to avoid creating a family and becoming a parent.

The loss of a parent in childhood or adolescence prompts one to think about the decision to have children. Having children creates the possibility of bringing familiar pain, of parent loss, into another child's life. In the absence of a parent, adults understand the importance of their parent's role in their life. In turn, they understand the importance of the role that they can fulfill in the life of their own child. These individuals gained an understanding that their own child will never understand—hopefully.

Intentional Presence in the Lives of Family Members

For a number of adults, this aspect of the loss represents the combined outgrowth of all other aspects, described throughout the previous chapters. Because it is the ultimate result of the loss for many people, it was appropriately placed at the end of this chapter. Based on a deep understanding of the importance of presence, and one's own familial changes, many adults develop a desire to be a presence in his or her own family.

As discussed in another chapter, adults felt that their loss taught them about the importance of being sensitive to others that have experienced loss. This aspect of the loss is about making a constant effort to be a presence in the lives of family members. Their loss has given them a sense of imminent mortality and an appreciation for life. Therefore, it is important to be *there* for loved ones, because death can happen at any time and any age.

Keeping Family as Top Priority

Family is the top priority in the lives of many adults interviewed for this book. Chuck explained that his career decisions have been based on his focus on his family:

> There have been a number of times in my career...I've been with my same company my whole career, which is unheard of...I've had numerous opportunities to manage this group or take this path, and I've always resisted...I'd be taking on responsibilities that could possibly take me away from my family...I'd rather dedicate whatever resources or energies I have to being the best dad that I can be.

Chad related his own view of family importance as a result of his loss. He also conveyed the message that he communicates to his children about the importance of family: "How important family was—we've always tried to instill that in our kids. They can go to school and they can make friends, but their friends are never going to love them the way their family's gonna love them." Although Blythe admitted that she can be standoffish to those who she is closest to, she said, "I will put family first when the chips are down."

Experiencing the early death of a parent often causes adults to place family responsibilities as their highest priority. A person who has experienced this loss knows what it feels like to have a family that was permanently changed or dissolved. They feel that this has taught them about what is truly important—family.

Using Experience to Guide Children

Besides a sense of familial closeness and prioritization, adults indicate that they want their own children to learn from their loss. Nancy said,

> What's really interesting is that I have one child—a daughter. I have parented her with teaching her some of those same independence skills. Not to say, "If for some reason I wasn't here, you could take care of yourself," but to help her always understand the way life is today: "You don't always have somebody to take care of you, so you have to assume roles."

Within her account is a pride in her daughter's development as a responsible person—something that seems to be an indirect result of her mother's loss. Nancy also said, "Life is unpredictable—not necessarily short—but unpredictable," which is an understanding that adults would like their children to grasp.

Knowing how to respond to others in loss is another beneficial lesson which adults are able to convey to their children. Nancy shared this story in which she was able to teach her daughter a basic lesson:

> When the father of my daughter's friend died, my daughter didn't know what to do... I told her to just write her a note—to just say something like, "I'm thinking of you." Learning how to be sensitive to people in their loss—that's really important.

To his children, Quinn explained his loss and the felt absence of his father. Out of his own understanding, he determined to "be there" for his children:

> I've talked to them. I've told them that part about not feeling love—and that would never happen to them... I told my son, "When we come home, anytime you want to play catch you just let me know and we'll have a ball with it." Even to my daughter, I've said, "Name any game you want, and we'll play."

Guiding their own children means teaching from their own lived experience with loss. The adult with the loss has been on a journey in which he or she has learned specific lessons. The understandings gained can then be used to teach valuable lessons to his or her children.

Passing on a Family History

In another chapter, sharing memories was briefly discussed as a way in which adults keep their parent present in memory. This example is different in that memories are a means to pass on family history to the next generation. In trying to give his son a history of his mother, Mike explained,

> You don't want to ever forget,...and that's scared me sometimes. I don't remember my mom sometimes. I've pulled out old pictures to show my son, and I've said, "This is your real grandmother. This is my mom."...Sometimes that chokes me up a little bit.

Vi said that although her children will never know her father, she continues to tell them about him. She explained her deliberate effort to communicate family history:

> They'll never know him, but yet I want...With our daughter, we really wanted her to understand that he was special and even though he's not in her life, he will be sorely missed. I want her to know where we came from, and I do not want him to be forgotten by the rest of the family. It's amazing how quickly a person can be forgotten in history.

Nancy also described her desire to continue a sense of family history:

> I still have written recipes in her handwriting that I've passed to my daughter. I think it's about understanding a sense of history. That is really important as we have

more divergent families—that we have some way to continue that line. Even if they aren't the living stories from the person themselves, at least we can pass that history through.

As disclosed in the previous examples, some adults make deliberate efforts to share memories of their deceased parent with their own children. Adults, who experienced the early death of a parent, serve as the only link between their parent and their children. Being a presence in their children's lives involves helping them understand their family history and the importance of presence.

Consciously Making Memories

An aspect of choosing to be a presence is expressed in a deliberate attempt to create memories. Olivia said, "I have learned that you should make proud memories every day because there may not be a tomorrow." Those adults with this loss are aware of the importance of making memories, especially in light of their understanding of imminent mortality. Chad said that his loss prompted him to think about the impact that he has on his children. He also said that he looks for opportunities to build special memories with his kids.

One way in which adults described their memory-making efforts was in the collection of pictures. Vi, an avid scrapbook maker, said this about her motivation:

> I know that I am conscious of making sure that there are pictures of my husband and me in our albums, and on videotape, so that the kids will have those someday. I have started putting together photo albums for the kids, so that they can each have their own set of pictures for later in life...If anything were to happen, there's something that I did for them. There are pictures of me, my handwriting, and my thoughts.

As described in previous chapters, adults such as Vi continue to recall a number of memories of their deceased parent, many years after their death. Many have pictures, but they don't reveal enough of the "story." As Vi creates photo albums for her children, she includes her thoughts. If she died tomorrow, she has intentionally left artifacts, in hopes that her children will know her better than she knows her deceased father. Her experience with the loss brought her to understand the importance of memories and to make them, as meaningful as possible, for her children.

Chuck expressed appreciation for the number of home movies that his father recorded in Chuck's childhood. He has one criticism of the movies: his father did most of the filming and is not often seen in the movies. Chuck is an avid photographer and videographer in his family. Although he admitted that he feels somewhat vain in doing it, he makes deliberate effort to be in front of the camera. If Chuck died tomorrow, his children would have visual and audio memories by which to remember him.

Mike expressed his sadness over the lack of memories he has of his mother. He also described a deliberate attempt to make memories for his son:

> I do a lot of things purposefully, with that whole idea that I want to create memories...What I want to do with my son, is create as many lasting memories as possible; from making puppets together; to playing hot wheels; to whatever. If I were to pass away, he'd never forget me.

The understandings that Quinn gained through his loss encouraged him to be very deliberate in his parenting. He described very close relationships between himself and his children. Those understandings became a lesson for parents about making memories: "And I tell parents now, 'It's too late at the casket. It's just way too late...You need to be building opportunities to make those memories, so make them.' "

The deliberate memory making is a continued feeling into grandparenthood, according to Quinn. His children are adults now, but he feels the need to create memories: "And that's what gets me out of a chair when my grandkids are out playing in the yard. I say, 'Lord, I gotta go make some memories.' " Quinn's presence in the lives of his grandchildren is something that he does not take for granted. It is also a part of life that few adults anticipate.

As described in other chapters, memories of a deceased loved-one are very important to the beholder, but most do not have an abundance of memories. What if a parent consciously made memories for their children? What if they did not? The loss of a parent emphasizes the importance of making memories in the lives of family members.

Looking Forward to Grandparenthood

Middle-aged adults, who experienced the early death of a parent, may anticipate grandparenthood. This anticipation represents relatively few of the individuals interviewed for this book, but it seems to be common among those whose children are in their late-teen or early-adult years. Grandparenthood is yet another way in which one may be intentional about being a presence in the lives of family members. As described in a previous chapter, most adults have been disappointed that their parent could not become a grandparent. At the same time, they may eventually look to their future roles as grandparents.

With each stage in life, Laura has hoped that she will live to the next. The next stage that she looks to is grandparenting: "I hope I'll live long enough so that I can be around my grandchildren." Sam said,

> Even now, I think about what it's going to be like having grand kids over here, and I kind of do things to that purpose... I wanted the place to be bigger so we all have room to gather... I plan like I'm going to be here a long time, but I could go quick... I think about what it's going to be like to be a grandpa—having a little kid on my lap and reading them a story or whatever...I want to be a grandpa that spends time with his grandkids and takes them on his lap and reads them a story.

In becoming a parent and a presence, adults fill a role for their children that their deceased parent did not completely fill for them. Becoming a grandparent seems to be an extension of that desire. In becoming a grandparent, one gives their grandchildren something that their children did not have—the presence of a grandparent. In both stages of life, the person works to be a presence in the life of family members.

Attending to Togetherness

Experiencing the death of a parent means living with separateness. The children are separated—cut off—from their parents. What is the opposite of separateness? The answer to that question is found in the efforts of adults who strive to be a presence in the lives of family members. The most common emphasis, which adults describe in connection with being a presence, was a focus on family togetherness. Many adults feel that they lost family togetherness after the early death of their parent. In response, they strive to create it anew in their families. Vi poignantly described this:

> My loss probably has given me such a strong sense to want to have a family that sticks together and stays together for many, many, many years—for the rest of our life. That's a good thing. To have a very strong sense of that... I probably go overboard on the family togetherness and closeness. I just don't want it to end... Part of it's a fear, but part of it is about wanting to do something together. I rarely want to be apart...

Forging a Relationship Together

An aspect of the absence of a parent is the absence of relationship. Adults, living with this loss, often place great importance on building relationships within their families. Chad said, "This relationship stuff is serious, important, and real business." Nancy explained her motivation for togetherness with her daughter:

It has been more to forge a richer relationship. It's hard,

because I think back....I only had twelve years of my mother's life...I think my emphasis on togetherness is probably done to forge a rich relationship because I think that's important.

For Quinn, having a family that would be emotionally connected was a dream that he worked to achieve:

I promised, in my soul, that my children would never experience a time when they didn't feel loved. Never!... I've been very deliberate—telling them all the time— even my daughter now that she's married—telling her that I'm so very proud of her.

Attending Milestones Together

As described in a previous chapter, adults describe the "big" moments as times in their lives in which they felt the absence of their parent. Laura, for example, conveyed a felt absence of her father in the milestone events of her life. She then expressed a desire to be there for the milestones in her sons' lives: "...that my kid would be able to...have their parents in the big things in life— throughout their life..." Once again, adults illustrate the use of the past to positively impact the present and future.

Making Time to be Together

Building togetherness takes time as well as effort. Although one may understand the importance of being present, making time to be together must be an intentional endeavor that often requires a sacrifice. Chad said his loss has helped him to understand the importance of spending time with his children:

I think of deliberateness, consciousness, being aware of, "Am I spending enough time with my kids?" ...It's not a given that I'm going to be around to see them another birthday or another Christmas. Those things aren't guaranteed, and you realize that when you lose a parent at a young age...You realize that you have, in the overall scheme of things, a relatively short period of time to instill your values...

As Chad learned through his loss, time is not a "given," and time is short. He also stressed the importance of sacrificing time for his children:

For me, I've always really felt like I pursued fatherhood. Some of it, I have to work at. I have to purposely spend time. I have to purposely go out of your way...When I'm sitting there, and my child walks over and wants to have a big, long conversation with me, and I'm in the middle of working, I have to consciously remember, "But they're important to me." ...So, it isn't always easy. But, I always have that in the back of my mind: "This is what life is about."

In conveying his feelings, Chad stated a phrase that accurately represents the heart of many people who experience the early death of a parent: "I pursued fatherhood." In other words, he dreamed, observed, learned, planned, and worked at fatherhood because, as he said, "This is what life is all about." Mike also spoke of being a presence by spending time together:

I try to spend as much time as I can with my son, pouring into him, and spending time with him, and doing things with him, because I don't know... Ten years from now I may be gone, and he may be without a dad. If that happens, I want to have poured into him as much as I can, so that he has a heritage...

Summary

What is it like to live with the loss of a parent who died in childhood or adolescence? It means being intentional in deciding whether to have a family. Those who decide to have a family are thoughtful and intentional in their presence in the lives of family members. These adults have developed specific ideas about what a family is and what a parent should be.

Personal Reflection

My personal reflections, related to this ninth chapter, were described in the first chapter and in various chapter summaries. In summary, my greatest God-given responsibilities are my greatest joys: loving my wife and loving and discipling my children. I am confident that my loss heightened my appreciation for my family and my responsibility to build a godly heritage for the generations to come.

My loss also prompted me to study family life, even as a teenager, which has blossomed into my ministry passion. The understanding, appreciation, and passion that I feel for family life, may not exist in my life without my loss.

For the Surviving Parent

• **Children should be encouraged to envision a life mission.** Their loss should not hinder them from doing what God wants them to accomplish. Instead, they can use it to God's glory. The surviving parent can instill this in their children by reminding, "You will do great things for God someday." This enables children to see beyond what they are missing to what they have to offer.

• **Children should be encouraged in their family plans.** Children may dream about the creation of their own family while they also doubt their own abilities to do so. They may be told that their loss has taken away any possibility of their being a successful parent or having a functional family. The surviving parent can assure their children that they will have an appreciation for family that is greater than the average person. Out of their loss, children may also develop an understanding that there is nothing more important—besides God—than family.

That the generation to come might know,
even the children yet to be born,
that they may arise and tell them to their children,
That they should put their confidence in God
and not forget the works of God,
but keep His commandments
Psalms 78:6-7

Chapter 10

Closing Reflections

For what purposes do people travel? Where do they go? People attend historical tours in Washington D. C.; they attend show tours in Branson, Missouri; and they attend natural history tours in Yellowstone National Park. Those who feel more adventurous may go cave exploring, scuba diving, or mountain climbing. Tours may take place in familiar or unfamiliar locations.

Encompassing the traits of all possible tours, life includes moments that are educational, entertaining, and inspirational. At times, life may be like a strenuous mountain climb; at other times it may be like a leisurely ride on a bus. In many cases, the presence of a guide is usually desired and needed.

What types of tour guides exist? What do people need from a tour guide? Depending on the type of tour, a guide may be responsible for disseminating information, demonstrating skills, or ensuring the safety and survival of the tourists. A guide may be responsible for steering a vehicle or leading a group of walking tourists in a specific direction. Tourists may also depend on the guide to find pathways in unexplored territory; lead the tourists by the hand when the trail is difficult; and light the path of the journey in order for the tourists to see where they are going. In any case, the tour guide is in a position of leadership, looked upon by the others for guidance.

The journey through life is a short tour from birth to death. Under normal circumstances, children are given parents who serve as the primary guides in their journey through life. Those adults interviewed for this book had a tour guide for only a short period of time, before experiencing that guide's premature, permanent departure. Whether emotionally close or disconnected from the parent, the early death of this vital person is a life-changing event. What is the child to do when life's challenges become as a dark cave, as a deep ocean, or as a steep mountain? Who will be their tour guide? Who will drive the bus and share the inspirational moments? Who will hold their hand in scary moments? Who will encourage them to press on when the journey seems impossible? Who will light their path when the journey becomes dark?

As a child grows, he or she continues to feel the impacts of the loss and the absence of the parent. Many of the life situations, described in the context of a tour or journey, are either faced alone, with the surviving parent, or with a surrogate parent. During the process of traveling, personal qualities of the individual develop in result of the parent's absence. Eventually, the child becomes an adult who continues to live with the loss and make decisions that are influenced by the loss—decisions that a tour guide may have made for them. Many endeavor to become tour guides, focused on guiding someone else through life—their own children. Their awareness of the unpredictability of the journey, and the possibility of death, urge many of them to be deliberate in their guiding.

Implications for Church Ministry

One may ask, "How can we focus on family togetherness and parenting ministries when we have children without parents?" I say, "How can we not?"

What if we balanced our age-based programs with a deliberate effort to use the family unit as an evangelism and discipleship tool? What if two-parent families operated as vehicles of outreach to single-parent families? Many families do not minister in such a way because churches do not operate this way. People have been conditioned to rely on age-segregated programs as the only way to do ministry.

After a boy or girl experiences the death of either parent, what is the best way for him or her to learn about being a spouse and parent—with families or with peers? The surviving parent can teach and model many qualities, but he or she cannot model the opposite role or relationship. If our only solution to meet the needs of families is through age-group ministries, we are sorely mistaken. Churches must minister to families—not just family members.

Children and teens who experience the death of a parent need ministry directed to their families. They also need to experience family-to-family ministry, which will equip them to build their own families in the future. As indicated by individuals in this book, adults who experienced the early death of a parent often rely upon their own observations and memories of others' parent-child and husband-wife relationships. Church should be the place where such modeling is deliberately done in order that future generations can learn how to build strong families.

What does this proposal for family ministry look like? It is seen in: a two-parent family that "adopts" a one-parent family for regular fellowship and fun; family small-groups that include two- and one-parent families; a father who regularly invites a fatherless boy to go fishing with he and his sons; a mother who invites a motherless daughter to go shopping; a group of men who welcome a fatherless boy to a men's breakfast; and a father who invites a fatherless daughter to an outing with he and his daughters. The possibilities are endless, but they communicate the same things: the love of Christ for every individual, support for families touched by loss, and hope for the future of strong families. Churches must facilitate such ministries in order that Jesus becomes apparent—and a parent—to those touched by the early death of a parent.

Summary.

What does it mean to live with the loss of a parent who died in one's childhood or adolescence? For some, it means a dependence on Jesus. He is present in the absence of a parent, and He is the only parent from whom we are never alone. Do you know what it means to trust Him with your losses and life direction? This song, *Where there Is Faith*, captures what it means to trust Jesus:

I believe in faithfulness,
I believe in giving of myself
For someone else.
I believe in peace and love,
I believe in honesty and trust,
But it's not enough.
For all that I believe will never change the way it is,
Unless I believe, that Jesus lives.
Where there is faith,
There is a voice calling,
"Keep walking. You're not alone in this world."
Where there is faith,
There is a peace like a child sleeping,
A Hope everlasting in He
Who is able to bare every burden,
To heal every hurt in my heart.
It is a wonderful, powerful place,
Where there is faith.
There's a man across the sea,
Never heard the sound of freedom ring,
Only in his dreams.
There's a lady dressed in black,
In a motorcade of Cadillacs.
Daddy's not coming back.
And our hearts begin to fall,
And our stability grows weak,
But Jesus meets our needs,
If we only believe,
Where there is faith,
There is a voice calling,
"Keep walking. You're not alone in this world."
Where there is faith,
There is a peace like a child sleeping

Hope everlasting in He
Who is able to bare every burden,
To heal every hurt in my heart.
It is a wonderful, powerful place,
Where there is faith... [1]

Perhaps you were a child that stood next to the "lady dressed in black" as you watched your parent's casket lower into the ground. Perhaps you were that lady, now responsible for helping your children on their journey without their daddy. The picture painted by those lines of the song may resemble an unfading memory of your own. Whether you were a child or the surviving parent in such a scene, you remember that day in which you said, "Good-bye."

The next line of the song reads, "Daddy's not coming back." There is finality in the death of a parent, but there is also hope for the future. As the truths in the chorus explain, the voice of God speaks to us; the presence of Jesus is with us; and peace and healing are offered to us. In the early death of a parent, God can become apparent—and a parent. I pray that you will trust Jesus with your life and loss. Have faith!

....

*And we know that God causes all things to work together
for good to those who love God,
to those who are called according to His purpose.
Romans 8:28*

Appendix 1

Existing Literature on the Early Death of a Parent

Few references to other resources were included in the chapters of this book, as life experiences were purposefully allowed to stand alone. This appendix is provided to expose the reader to the scope of previously-written research on the death of a parent in one's childhood or adolescence. This appendix includes an examination of a few basic themes of this book in relation to other literature. The second appendix is an extended review of other literature on this topic.

This book is not an exact description of the experiences of every person living with this loss. A similar book, including the same loss and involving different adults in interviews, may include additional themes not found in this book. At the same time, another book, with different participants, may not uncover the same themes described in this work.

Much of existing literature on this subject involves the examination of cause-and-effect relationships in the lives of individuals who experienced the death of a parent in childhood or adolescence. In contrast, this book includes deep understandings directly from the words of individuals who know what it is like to experience, feel, and live with this lifelong loss. Nevertheless, it is important to examine the relation between this work and other literature.

What does the literature say in relation to the loss? How do existing studies relate to this book? Of importance to this study is what the literature already includes, but of greater importance is what the existing literature does not say. With exception of a few books, most of existing literature does not include how the death of a parent in childhood or adolescence is lived out. It does not often address the meaning of the experience in a deep, profound way. It does not often point to what it means to experience this loss.

Most studies, within existing literature, involve a narrow focus on one aspect of the loss. A number of works also include discussions of related themes such as grief, death, and loss. The following sections include aspects of existing literature that are seen in this book.

Main Themes and Sub-Themes of This Study

As previously discussed, adults described their loss as a marker between two lives. In this theme, they emphasized the magnitude of the life-altering event. Heinzer (1995) wrote, "Parental death in childhood is considered a major loss, one that could have a serious impact on adaptation in adolescence and later adulthood." According to adults interviewed for this book, this major loss seriously impacted the future. C. S. Lewis (1961) explained that grief is so frustrating because the griever cannot continue in the same impulses and habits, because the object of those impulses is gone. He also said that many roads, once leading to that person, are turned into cul-de-sacs (p. 60). In a similar way, individuals' lives were profoundly changed when access to a parent was taken away.

Adults also described living with childhood memories of their loss. Wessel (1996) recognized this in his pediatric practice: "I discovered that many expectant parents had suffered the loss of a parent during childhood. I was surprised that many men and women cried as they shared memories of their losses during the first decade of their life" (p. 77). Wright (1993) said, "We all perceive life from our backlog of experiences because our memories are always with us" (p. 31). Adults exhibited a similar use of memories. When asked to describe living with their loss, they most often started with their memories from the early years with the loss.

Within the descriptions of their childhood memories, were adults' recollections of childhood grief. They described what they learned about grief and grieving, which included being alone in their grief and looking for cues from adults. James and Friedman (1998) said that grief is the most misunderstood experience, often by both the grievers and those around them. Nuttall (1997) said, "Children grieve and their grief needs and deserves acknowledgement. To do things that make them feel that their loss and sadness are inferior to other people's grief will be unhelpful and may hinder their own grieving" (p. 95). Adults described similar scenarios in dealing with their own grief and looking to those around them for guidance. Like many children with this loss, the people in this study were often excluded from the collective grieving process.

As discussed in another chapter, adults described ways in which they have viewed their loss through adult eyes. Simon and Drantell (1998) wrote, "...losing a parent to death in childhood is a life event that keeps on reverberating long into adulthood" (p. 17). As the reverberation continues, different understandings occur in adulthood. Wright (1993) said, "Whenever a loss occurs, it is important to see it in the context of your life experiences so you understand the full impact of what has happened" (p. 20). The adults in this study described a similar development of their understandings that occurred in adulthood—years after the death of their parent—in the context of adult life.

Another main theme described by adults was the felt absence of the deceased parent throughout life. Their loss is a forever loss of which they are often reminded. Kopp (1998) wrote "Eventually, you will no longer actively grieve your father-loss. In another sense, you may never stop. In fact, just when you think you'll never shed another tear, an older man who reminds you of your father might come along and make you cry" (p. 101). Adults described such unexpected moments in which they felt the absence of their deceased parent.

In a related theme of meaning, adults described a sense that their deceased parent remains present in memory throughout life. As disclosed in adults' descriptions, remembering the parent is of great importance. Adults included thoughts of having their parent frozen in time, also seen in a study by Dietrich and Shabad (1989), and idealizing their parent, also seen in a study by Richter, Eisemann, Richter, and Perris (1992).

Research is supported by the theme of having the deceased parent in memory. Silverman, Nickman, and Worden (1992) explained that a connection is maintained in an effort to make sense of the loss. Rosenblatt and Elde (1990) said that grief work may include keeping connections with memories of the deceased. Silverman et al. (1992) also recognized that memorializing may continue throughout the child's life as a way to make sense of the meaning of the parent in his or her life. They stated, "In this process, the child seeks to gain not only an understanding of the meaning of death, but a sense of the meaning of this now-dead parent in his or her life" (p. 502). Such a process was evident in this book, within adults' descriptions of living with their loss.

Adults also expressed understanding and defining themselves in relation to their loss. As Emswiler and Emswiler (2000) wrote, "Speak with anyone who lost a parent as a child, and they'll tell you the experience contributed significantly to forming their identity. For adolescents and young adults, it may be the only self-definition they have" (p. 195). Lohnes and Kalter (1994) recognized that children often need to maintain an emotional attachment to the deceased parent in order to promote personality development. Adults in this book described an effort to understand themselves in relation to the impact of their deceased parent.

Understanding the Lived Experience

Wolpe (1999) said, "The blessing we seek in life is not to live without pain. It is to live so that our pain has meaning" (p. 12). Adults in this study had an early encounter with pain. They learned that life is unpredictable and loss is inevitable. Along with these learned realities was an effort to understand their loss.

In *Motherless Daughters*, Hope Edelman (1994) explored a

number of themes. Here are a few: familial change and the connections and disconnections often involved with the loss; a girl's need for a woman and mother; the effect of the loss on intimate relationships; development of an independent identity; mortal lessons; a daughter's approach to motherhood; and the development of a successful woman.

In her last chapter, Edelman (1994) wrote about feeling unique; journeying alone; honoring the deceased parent; searching for immortality; creating meaning of the loss. These themes, along with the last four themes in the previous paragraph, are particularly consistent with the themes of meaning in this work. Her other themes are not discounted by this book, but they were not found to be common understandings of the phenomenon among the adults in this study.

Edelman (1994) wrote about the determination of individuals to live with their loss by striving for success in life. While this work does not include this specific theme, an overall sense of heightened maturity, responsibility, and independence was observed in adults. For many, this sense led to the achievement of various successes in life. Edelman wrote,

> It appears that children who lose a parent generally respond in one of two ways: they develop a sense of fatalism, expecting and even encouraging future unfortunate events to occur, or they pick themselves up, brush themselves off, and find the determination and motivation to continue. (p. 260)

The latter were most prominent among the adults of this study.

Another book about the overall experience of living with the early death of a parent was written by Maxine Harris (1995). Slightly different from this book, which is focused on common meanings of the lived experience, Harris's book was focused upon individuals and the many possible impacts of the loss on their lives. Yet, similarities between the two books are evident. The following themes within Harris's book are those which are similar to themes uncovered in this book. She wrote about: the event that shatters childhood; mythology about the deceased parent; fantasy about the relationship that might have been; creating the self; childless by choice; parenting without a model; the fear of death; staying in touch with the deceased parent through objects and rituals; and owning one's destiny.

What Existing Literature Does Not Say

Existing literature includes a number of aspects of parent loss, but it does not often include how the death of a parent in childhood or adolescence is experienced and lived out into adulthood. This book provides understandings for both the childhood impacts of this loss and it's implications in adulthood. The uniqueness of the study was explained in early chapters, but it is important, at the conclusion of this book, to reemphasize differences. The following paragraphs include a sampling of what was described in this study but absent from existing literature.

A large portion of existing research on this subject has been devoted to the resiliency and adaptive efforts of children or adolescents who experience the death of a parent. Studies have involved a variety of conclusions based on short-term and long-term challenges, such as depression, anxiety, behavioral problems, unsociability, and physical and mental health problems. This study was not designed to measure such challenges but to capture the essence of the overall life experience.

As indicated in existing literature, concepts dominate the research related to the early death of a parent. Within studies of challenges and resiliency are a number of concepts into which subjects are categorized. While such research provides valuable information, it is void of a vital aspect of understanding: the life and experience of the individual. Whether in the life of a child, adolescent, or adult, adapting to and coping with this loss is best described in one's own words.

This book points to the lived experience of individuals. In relation to the challenges and resiliency of people in this book, adults described the importance of others, the lessons they learned about grieving, and the ways in which they have chosen to live with their loss. These descriptions helped to explain the loss with a human touch.

What does it mean to live with the death of a parent that occurred in childhood or adolescence? Existing research does not often address the meaning of this experience in a deep way. It does not often point to what it means to be human and live with the death of a parent. This book was written in order to discover such meanings and use them in describing the experience. As previously alluded to, much of existing research in this area involves the fine parsing of variables to achieve understanding. While valuable, the research is often missing an important focus: a deep and profound understanding of the experience.

Appendix 2

An Extended Review of Literature

This appendix is an in-depth overview of literature that has been written about the early death of a parent. It does not include connections to this book, as described in the previous appendix.

Besides not receiving affirmation that their grief is real, Rando (1988) explained that children are disadvantaged as grievers. One very important way is that children are immature in their understanding. She said,

> Also, because of their intellectual immaturity and lack of experience, children tend not to have the words to describe their feelings, thoughts, or memories, which is so important in grief resolution. This should not surprise you. You know how overwhelming and confusing grief is; it is sometimes difficult for you yourself to identify thoughts and words that can help you manage your own feelings of grief. This is even more the case for children. (p. 200)

She also explained that children are disadvantaged as grievers because they tend to take things literally, especially in their understanding of one being "lost"; they do not have access to resources to help them cope; they do not always have the experience to know that they can survive the loss; they do not have a great capacity to tolerate pain over time; they may wait until they are sure that their needs are going to be met before they give in to grieving; their parents may not understand that children's play is often their way to work through grief; and they have adults that deny them opportunities to grieve, in an effort to protect them (pp. 200-202).

The main focus of Rando's (1988) work includes ways in which adults can help children through the grief attached to the death of a parent. Emswiler and Emswiler (2000) published such a work. They explained how parents and other adults can communicate with a grieving child in such a way that they are helping the child. For example, their advice included: listen with empathy; don't interrupt; acknowledge the child's feelings with words and gestures; be honest; be as factual as the age requires; be patient; avoid figurative language; revisit and recommunicate.

There are also many books that include an approach to this topic through the description of personal accounts and meanings. After losing her husband, Teakle (1992) wrote about her own daughters' journeys through the grief of their loss. Krementz (1981) compiled the stories of eighteen different children and adolescents who experienced the death of a parent. As one reads these individual accounts, one can't help but notice the clarity with which the children speak of their memories. A number of books exist in relation to this specific loss. Many of them offer valuable insights into understanding and helping children in their grief of losing a parent.

Although this book does not focus on the gender of the child or parent as a main purpose of discovery, it is important to recognize that such gender specificity exists within the literature. Harold Ivan Smith (1994) compiled a book that includes the recollections of many famous and not-so-famous people, on the passing, burying, mourning, and remembering of their fathers. Smith said,

As I read through passages written by sons and daughters, I found different responses to their father's death—from syndicated humor columnist Lewis Grizzard's submerged grief to author Frederick Buechner's amazement at his father's suicide to author Carolyn Koons's mixed emotions after the death of a father who had abused her to author Tim Hansel's feelings of love and peace. (p. 39)

Heather Harpham Kopp (1998) wrote in order to deal with her own father-loss issues and help others do the same. She dealt with such issues as: recognizing her attempt to fill the father-void, with other men; experiencing mother-loss simultaneously with the death of a father, as a mother becomes withdrawn; sharing father-loss among siblings; dealing with the life-long loss. Kopp's book contains many important insights.

Another gender-related aspect in the literature exists in a focus on the survivor. Staudacher (1991), who specifically focused on men, said, "When a man describes his boyhood reactions after the loss of his parent or sibling, he'll usually say something similar to this: 'I withdrew. I kept everything to myself. I didn't show what I was feeling' " (p. 52). On this subject and the unrealistic societal expectations placed on grieving men, Kuenning (1987) wrote:

The male is expected to be more resilient and able to control his feelings. These expectations may inhibit a man from openly expressing his grief. It should be clearly understood that both men and women experience the shock, the anger, guilt and loneliness, and depression that accompanies bereavement. When forced to suffer in silence, a man's pain can become unbearable for him and produce an inner rage. (p. 217)

Keunning's view is supported by literature. Staudacher (1991) recorded the words of a forty-year-old survivor who was sixteen when his father died: "I withdrew my emotions, kept them to myself, cried by myself. Whenever I was alone, I kind of let it out. I didn't really share my true feelings with my friends, my intense grief and sense of loss..." (p. 52).

Experimental Research

Research journals also make up a large portion of grief literature that is focused upon children's experiences with the death of a parent. Most of these works include ways to help children or teens after their parent has died. Many of these studies, just as the books previously mentioned, have been written in the past twenty years. Most of them are located in psychiatric and medical journals.

A number of studies have focused primarily on grief in the adolescent who experiences the death of a parent. Kuntz (1990) explored how adolescents grieve after the death of a parent. She found that adolescents proceeded through grief in their own ways, according to a timetable dictated by their own situation, personality, and circumstances. Heinzer (1995) studied adolescent resilience after parental death in childhood and its relationship to attachment and coping. She found that exogenous variables, such as age, length of time since parental death, and circumstance of death, were not significant predictors of resilience. Instead, adaptive coping with self and environment was a strong predictor of resilience.

Marwit and Carusa (1996) examined the experiences of parental death and parental divorce in adolescence. Few differences were found between death and divorce survivor groups. Death and divorce are both traumatic events for adolescents.

Mourning and Adaptive Efforts

Although it may seem like an obvious assumption, research has shown that the quality of the parent-child relationships both before and after the death are important determinants of long-term adaptation to the loss (Bilfulco, Harris, & Brown, 1992; Breier, Kelsoe, Kerwin, Beller, Wolkowitz, & Pickar, 1988; Elizur & Kaffman, 1983). The stability of the family and the availability of support for the children and surviving parent are also determinants (Elizur & Kaffman, 1983; Silverman & Worden, 1992).

Grace Hyslop Christ (2000) wrote about assisting adults in helping children through the grief of losing a parent to cancer. She combined quantitative and qualitative research methods as she examined families among various age ranges of children (3-5, 6-8, 9-11, 12-14, 15-17). Christ specifically explored the differences in children's mourning processes and their adaptive efforts in living life without a parent. She found that developmental differences in mourning existed between the age-levels of children. Perhaps her most important findings dealt with the children's reconstitution to "normal" life, affected by the surviving parent and other factors:

> These analyses showed that most surviving parents, both fathers and mothers, could be helpful, supportive, and encouraging to their children in many different ways that contributed to the children's timely or delayed reconstitution...even parents with major psychiatric disorders could deal with their difficulties so that their children experienced a timely or delayed reconstitution...the most striking finding was the many factors that were different in each child's environment, rather than the death alone, seemed to be most powerfully associated with these outcomes. (p. 242)

Erma Furman has been involved with the study of children's bereavement for many years. Her name is found throughout the literature, especially in connection with her early work, *A Child's Parent Dies: Studies in Childhood Bereavement* (1974). A group of child psychoanalysts studied twenty-three children who experienced parent death. Furman (1974, 1983) explained the six factors that these professionals observed as helpful practices to master bereavement: having good emotional health prior to the event; understanding the death, its cause and circumstances, and burial; hoping for continued life for self; mourning; resuming the process of living; receiving help from the surviving parent or a parent-substitute (pp. 243-246).

While these findings are generally consistent with the literature, other specific issues are addressed throughout studies, including comparisons between bereaved and non-bereaved children, differences between short-term and long-term effects, and issues of recollection.

In a study of eighty-three families, with school age children, in which a parent died of cancer, Raveis, Siegel, and Karus (1999) strove to understand predictors of children's adjustment to the loss. They found that the child's perception of the surviving parent's level of openness, in parental communication, was found to be significant in lower levels of depressive symptoms. Results also showed that boys reported lower levels of depressive symptoms than did girls.

Research has also drawn attention to children's recollections of the deceased parent. In the study by Richter, Eisemann, Richter, and Perris (1992), children were observed as holding global idealizations of their deceased parents, especially when compared to other diagnostic groups that experienced parent loss by divorce. Research has indicated that the child mourner must disengage from the deceased parent in order for successful mourning to take place (Furman, 1974, 1984). As mentioned in the previous section of this appendix, researches have seen the child's attempt to maintain a connection to a dead parent as an important practice. It is often an active effort to make sense of the experience of loss and to make it part of the child's reality.

Effects of the Loss

Research literature that is focused upon examining the effects of parent death in childhood, has linked the loss of a parent, in childhood or adolescence, to a variety of short-term challenges (Berlinsky & Biller, 1982; Elizur & Kaffman, 1983; Osterweis, Solomon, & Green, 1984; Van Eerdewegh, Bieri, Parilla, & Clayton, 1982). Literature also indicates that children can experience related challenges in development years after a parent dies (Berlinsky & Biller, 1982; Brown, Harris, & Bilfulco, 1986; Elizur & Kaffman, 1983; Finkelstein, 1988; Gay & Tonge, 1967; Lohnes & Kalter, 1994; Osterweis et al., 1984; Van Eerdewegh et al., 1982; Worden & Silverman, 1996). A number of these effects and challenges are included in the following sections.

Compared With Non-Bereaved Children

Siegel, Karus, and Raveis (1996) studied the resilience of children who have lost a parent. They found, while many children were experiencing the loss of a parent to cancer, reported elevated levels of depression and anxiety existed before the parent's death. By seven to twelve months after their parent's death, their reports of depression and anxiety were comparable with those of similarly situated children in the community, who did not experience such a loss. This indicates that many children have a resiliency after a parent's death, but it does not negate the fact that life is changed forever and loss still exists.

Another study compared bereaved children with both depressed children and non-depressed children (Fristad, Jadel, Weller, & Weller, 1993). Findings indicated that the bereaved children functioned significantly better than depressed children. Also, functioning at school, interacting with peers, and self-esteem were not significantly affected in bereaved children from stable families. Once again, although adaptability seemed to be achieved in many of these children, they would be faced with the loss throughout the remainder of their lives.

Worden and Silverman (1996) found that there were significant emotional/ behavioral differences between bereaved, school-age children and their non-bereaved controls (social withdrawal, anxiety, lower self-esteem and self-efficacy). These findings did not occur until two years after the deaths. Brennan and Shaver (1998) also found that individuals with deceased parents were more likely to be unsociable than were individuals whose parents were both still living. Another study, by Thompson, Kaslow, Kingree, King, Bryant, and Rey (1998), was done with predominantly minority children. The researchers studied a sample of eighty bereaved and forty-five nonbereaved youth. Results revealed that bereaved youth had greater psychological and behavior problems than their nonbereaved counterparts.

Related to Stress

Lohnes and Kalter (1994) found that children struggle with death-related stress, well beyond the time of the loss. As they explained,

> Most of the themes that surfaced were not directly related to the loss itself, but to the ongoing adjustment necessary after the death...while children in the group expressed psychic pain and evidenced defenses against such expressions, they also made it clear that there is as much work to be done in adjusting to the stresses of the aftermath as there is in coping with the pain of the death itself. (p. 602)

Affects on Physical and Mental Processes

As the research literature increases, so does the variety of findings. In relation to how parental loss in childhood can affect physical and mental processes, a number of different findings exist. Luecken (1998) found that both childhood loss of a parent and poor quality of caretaking are associated with long-term increases in blood pressure and altered neurohormonal responses to stress. In a different study, Luecken (2000) found that parental loss in childhood is often associated with health-damaging, psychosocial characteristics in adulthood—only if the quality of the surviving, family relationship is poor. Yet another study suggested that genetic predisposition may influence the susceptibility of an individual to the negative effects of early parent loss (Agid, Shapira, Zislin, Ritsner, Hanin, Murad, Troudart, Bloch, Heresco-Levy, & Lerer, 1999).

Much of the research, which has been focused upon the long-term effects of persons bereaved in childhood, has shown that children often experience psychological challenges. Dilworth and Hildreth (1997) expressed otherwise:

> ...Past research has failed to confirm that parental death results in pervasive psychological disturbance in the absence of certain mediating factors (e.g., genetic predisposition). The largest group of early parental death

survivors [in this study] clearly exists in the normative, non-psychiatric population. (p. 155)

Gender Differences

A number of studies observed gender differences in the childhood loss of a parent. Among forty-five bereaved families with children, aged two to sixteen years, Dowdney, Wilson, Maughan, Allerton, Schofield, and Skuse (1999) discovered that parentally bereaved children, and surviving parents, showed higher than expected levels of psychiatric difficulties. Boys were more affected than girls, and bereaved mothers had more mental health difficulties than bereaved fathers. Maier and Lachman (2000) examined the impact of parental death and divorce, which occurred before age seventeen, on physical and mental well-being. The sample consisted of middle-aged adults. They found that parental death predicted more autonomy for men and a higher likelihood of depression for women. Knight, Elfenbein, and Capozzi (2000) found that boys and girls do not respond differently to the first death experience. However, there seemed to be a gender relation in regard to the connection between the adults' first death experience and their current death attitudes. Boys remembered their experience with a more negative attitude about death.

Secondary Stressors

The loss of a parent in childhood often has other losses attached to it. These are recognized, by many, as primary and secondary losses. Thompson, Kaslow, Price, Williams, and Kingree (1998) examined various psychological consequences and secondary stressors associated with the death of a parent. Reports indicated that parent death was associated with an increase in secondary stressors, regardless of how the parent died. In children that experienced the death of both parents, secondary losses, especially isolation, exacerbated the bereavement processes (Mahon, 1999). Each loss, whether primary or secondary, can have a profound effect on an individual. The early death of a parent will also have a number of different losses connected to it.

Anticipatory Loss and Grief

Family members of terminally-ill patients often begin the process of grieving before actual death occurs (Lindemann, 1944). Children of these patients, as well as other family members, are faced with the possibility of prolonged anxiety, agony, uncertainty, ambivalence, and guilt (Aldrich, 1974). Roshenheim and Reicher (1986) examined the anxiety of such children and their parents. They determined,

> It is a sad fact that society does little to provide them with a psychosocial framework that will guide them through the emotional maze of this stage. Children and parents in anticipatory grief do not receive a normative perspective to perplexing feelings and alternatives of action similar to those offered in actual mourning. (p. 119)

The authors also encouraged mental health workers to become forerunners in this area.

Findings related to anticipatory grief seem to vary. A study of parentally bereaved children demonstrated that a forewarning of death is not associated with more favorable mental health outcomes than the sudden death of a parent (Saldinger, Cain, Kalter, & Lohnes, 1999). One study recognized the favorable, coping abilities that adolescents often develop at such a time (Christ, Siegel, & Sperber, 1994), while other researchers explained, "…for the children of terminally ill parents, the months immediately prior to the death entail greater psychological vulnerability than what is traditionally regarded as the period of grieving" (Tremblay & Israel, 1998, p. 431).

Intervention

Variety also exists among the grief literature focused on intervention. Zambelli, Clark, Barile, and Jong (1988) explained that a creative arts approach may be an effective intervention for facilitating mourning experiences for children. They also stressed that grief therapy must be done with the entire family for resolution to occur: "Initial observations suggest that the grieving child must be considered in the context of his or her family system and that the value of the therapy is redoubled when offered as part of an interdisciplinary intervention" (p. 49). Mulcahey and Young (1995) explained that in bereavement support, time-limited groups are therapeutic because they have a beginning, middle, and end. This provides children and other family members with a predictable experience in a time when the unpredictability of life has been experienced.

Differences of Opinion

It may be valuable for the reader to understand the differences of opinion that exist in research. Journal articles, such as the many reviewed in this appendix, usually offer findings that establish solid conclusions. On the other hand, studies seem to prove opposite findings on the same subject. Harrington and Harrison (1999) challenged a number of the conclusions found in research. These findings are what the authors believed to be unproven assumptions of childhood bereavement literature: bereavement is a major risk factor for mental disorder in children; childhood bereavement often leads to depression in adulthood; bereaved children must accomplish a sequence of grieving tasks; bereaved children and their families will often benefit from professional help; bereavement counseling cannot do any harm (pp. 230-231).

Experiential Writing

One of the most popular books on parental loss is Hope Edelman's (1994) *Motherless Daughters*. Edelman dealt with a specific loss that is filled with specific challenges. She said, "All daughters—and motherless ones are no exception—expect mothers to pass down the generational knowledge that transforms a girl into a woman" (p. 179). Without that important relationship, daughters can often feel that they never learned what they needed to know.

The themes found in Edelman's work were included in the previous section of this appendix.

Two other books, which include gender-specific examinations of the loss of a parent, are Chethik's (2001) *Fatherloss* and Davidman's (2000) *Motherloss*. Obvious in their titles, these books include a focus on losing a gender-specific parent. Davidman (2000) specifically explored the experiences of men and women who had lost their mothers between the ages of ten and fifteen. She chose this age range to ensure that clear memories and a number of growing-up years existed in the lives of the adults. Davidman focused primarily on ten respondents, whose lengthy narratives are presented throughout the book. Her work, much like *Motherless Daughters* (1994), includes a focus on same-gender parent loss. Davidman's work is quite different in age range, participant selection, theme development, and writing style. Chethik (2001) examined ways in which sons of all ages come to terms with the death of their fathers. He surveyed three-hundred men and interviewed seventy who experienced the death of their fathers in a wide range of ages. In the first chapter, Chethik focused on the same age-range used in this study (birth to seventeen years old).

Simon and Drantell (1998) examined childhood bereavement and its effects on adults that experienced the early death of a parent. The authors interviewed seventy individuals whose responses were grouped into themes. The result was a compilation of many themes tied together by oral histories. Their work points to shared themes while emphasizing the uniqueness of each experience.

Appendix 3

People and Their Descriptions

Quotes for the book came from interviews and written accounts of adults who had experienced the death of a parent in childhood or adolescence. The criteria for including individuals was that each participant was in his or her adult years and had experienced the death of a parent in childhood or adolescence. No attempt was made to differentiate between family structures, cause of death, gender of the participant, or gender of the deceased parent. With the assistance of email and the recommendations of others, potential adults contacted the researcher. Third-party contacts invited individuals to make the initial contact.

Twenty individuals participated in face-to-face interviews—ten men and ten women. The age range of the group ranged from twenty-three to seventy-six years of age. The age at which they experienced their parent's death ranged from two months to seventeen years of age. Although not planned to be evenly distributed, ten adults experienced the death of a mother, and ten experienced the death of a father.

Twenty additional adults were included by way of written

accounts. The written accounts used in this study were original texts. Most writings were rich in meaning, even when they consisted of a few sentences. The age range of the group was from about twenty to fifty years of age. The age at which they experienced their parent's death ranged from three to seventeen years of age. Thirteen adults experienced the death of a mother, and seven experienced the death of a father.

The majority of adults in this study were American-born individuals. Therefore, the general context of their experience is American culture, which may differ from other cultures, in significant ways, regarding the death of a parent. For example, within other cultures, nuclear family units may not be as autonomous as those in American culture.

Of the adults that communicated through email, the amount of generated text varied from one paragraph to twenty pages. They were asked to answer the basic question with any length of answer: "What does it mean for you to live with the loss experienced through the death of your parent in childhood or adolescence?" In order to help them understand the question, they were asked to focus on key understandings such as experience, meaning, and living with the loss.

Interviews were the primary means of hearing the stories of others. Each interview began with a variation of the primary question, "What has it been like for you to live with the loss experienced from the death of a parent in your childhood or adolescence?" Subsequent questions were based upon the conversation. Interviews were recorded on a digital recorder, and every word was transcribed. Transcriptions and written accounts were hermeneutically analyzed and used to determine the main themes of the experience.

Notes

Introduction

1. <u>Merriam-Webster Collegiate dictionary</u> (2000). [online dictionary]. Available: www.m-w.com [October 28, 2000].
2. Bowman, T. (Instructor). (1999). <u>Shattered Dreams</u> (class). St. Paul, MN: University of Minnesota.
3. Wolfelt, A. D. (1997). <u>Dispelling 5 common myths about grief</u> [online article]. Available: www.messenger.org/ComMes97/Mesjan97/Mesjan05.htm [January 11, 2001]. (p. 2).
4. Bowman, T. (1994). <u>Loss of dreams: A special kind of grief.</u> St. Paul, MN: Ted Bowman. (p. 4).
5. Bowman, T. (1994). <u>Loss of dreams: A special kind of grief.</u> St. Paul, MN: Ted Bowman. (p. 12).
6. Mitchell, K., & Anderson, H. (1983). <u>All our losses; All our griefs.</u> Philadelphia: The Westminster Press, 1983.
7. Bowman, T. (1994). <u>Loss of dreams: A special kind of grief.</u> St. Paul, MN: Ted Bowman. (p. 12).
8. Rando, T. (1993). <u>Treatment of complicated mourning.</u> Champaign, IL: Research Press.
9. Silverman, P., & Worden, W. (1992). Children's reactions in the early months after the death of a parent. <u>American Journal of Orthopsychiatry, 62,</u> 93-104.
10. Wessel, M. A. (1996). When children mourn a loved one. In H. M. Spiro, M. G. McCrea Curnen, & L. P. Wandel (Eds.),

Facing death. New Haven, CT: Yale University Press. (p. 77).
11. Heinzer, M. M. (1995). Loss of a parent in childhood: Attachment and coping in a model of adolescent resilience. Holistic Nursing Practice, 9, (3), 27-37.
12. Furman, E. (1983). Studies in childhood bereavement. Canadian Journal of Psychiatry, 28 (4), 241-247. (p. 242).
13. Dietrich, D. R., & Shabad, P.C. (1989). The problem of loss and mourning. Madison, CT: international Universities Press.
14. Rosenblatt, P., & Elde, C. (1990). Shared reminiscence about a deceased parent: Implications for grief education and grief counseling. Family Relations, 39, 206-210.
15. Simon, L., & Drantell, J. J. (1998). A music a no longer heard. New York, NY: Simon & Schuster. (p. 17).
16. Wright, H. N. (1993). Recovering from the losses of life. Grand Rapids, MI: Fleming H. Revell. (p. 27).
17. Wright, H. N. (1993). Recovering from the losses of life. Grand Rapids, MI: Fleming H. Revell. (p. 31).
18. Wright, H. N. (1993). Recovering from the losses of life. Grand Rapids, MI: Fleming H. Revell. (p. 20).
19. Hickman, M. W. (1994). Healing after loss: Daily meditations for working through grief. New York, NY: Avon Books, Inc. (p. 290).
20. Grollman, E. A. (1995). Living when a loved one has died. Boston, MA: Beacon Press. (p. 2).

Chapter 1
1. Our Daily Bread (H. Bosch, Editor.). (December, 1980). Grand Rapids, MI: Radio Bible Class.
2. Our Daily Bread (H. Bosch, Editor.). (December, 1980). Grand Rapids, MI: Radio Bible Class.
3. Zucker, J., Rubin, B., Lowry, H. (Producer), & Ruben, B. (Director). (1994). My life. [Movie]. Burbank, CA: Columbia Pictures.
4. Edelman, H. (1994). Motherless daughters. New York, NY: Delta Publishing. (pp. 274-275).

Chapter 3
1. Chapman, G., & Campbell, R. (1997). <u>The five love languages of children.</u> Chicago, IL: Moody Press.

Chapter 6
1. <u>Random House College dictionary</u> (5th ed.). (1984). New York, NY: Random House.
2. Webster, N. (1828). <u>American dictionary of the English language</u> (1st ed. reprint). San Francisco, CA: Foundation for American Christian Education.
3. <u>Random House College dictionary</u> (5th ed.). (1984). New York, NY: Random House.
4. <u>Random House College dictionary</u> (5th ed.). (1984). New York, NY: Random House.

Chapter 7
1. <u>Random House College dictionary</u> (5th ed.). (1984). New York, NY: Random House.
2. <u>Random House College dictionary</u> (5th ed.). (1984). New York, NY: Random House.
3. Dubs, A. (Producer), & Raffill, S. (Director). (1975). <u>The Adventures of the wilderness family.</u> [Movie]. United American Video Corporation.

Chapter 8
1. Chapman, S. C. (2001). God is God. On <u>Declaration</u> [CD]. Brentwood, TN: Sparrow Records.
2. Spielberg, S., Canton, N., & Gale, B. (Producers), & Zemeckis, R. (Director). (1995). <u>Back to the future.</u> [Movie]. MCA Pictures.
3. Wright, H. N. (1993). <u>Recovering from the losses of life.</u> Grand Rapids, MI: Fleming H. Revell. (p. 33).
4. Wright, H. N. (1993). <u>Recovering from the losses of life.</u> Grand Rapids, MI: Fleming H. Revell. (p. 36).
5. Gallin, S., Orr, J., Cruickshank, J., & Williams, C. (Producers), & Shyer, C. (Director). (1991). <u>Father of the bride.</u> [Movie]. (1991). Touchstone Pictures.

6. Frankish, B., Gordon, L., & Gordon, C. (Producers), & Robinson, P. A. (Director). (1989). Field of dreams. [Movie]. Universal Studios.
7. McLaglen, M., Bullock, S., & Obst, L. (Producers), & Whitaker, F. (Director). (1998). Hope floats. [Movie]. Twentieth Century Fox Films.
8. Redmond, D. (Athlete). (1992). Derrick Redmond: 1992 Olympics. [Stock Footage]. Colorado Springs, CO: U.S. Olympic Committee Broadcasting.

Chapter 10
1. 4 Him. (1997). Where there is faith. On 4 Him. [CD]. Nashville, TN: Benson Music Group.

Appendices (*Alphabetically Listed*)
Agid, O., Shapira, B., Zislin, J., Ritsner, M., Hanin, B., Murad, H., Troudart, T., Bloch, M., Heresco-Levy, U., & Lerer, B. (1999). Environment and vulnerability to major psychiatric illness: a case control study of early parental loss in major depression, bipolar disorder and schizophrenia. Molecular Psychiatry, 4, 163-172.

Aldrich, C. K. (1974). Some dynamics of anticipatory grief. In B. Schoenberg, A. C. Carr, A. H. Kutscher, D. Peretz, & I. K. Goldberg (Eds.), Anticipatory grief (pp. 3-10). New York, NY: Columbia University Press.

Bauman, H. (1973). Grief's slow work. Scottdale, PA: Herald Press.
Berlinsky, E., & Biller, H. (1982). Parental death and psychological development. Lexington, MA: Lexington Books.

Bilfulco, A., Harris, T., & Brown, G. (1992). Mourning or early inadequate care? Reexamining the relationship of maternal loss in childhood with adult depression and anxiety. Development and Psychopathology, 4, 433-449.

Breier, A., Kelsoe J., Kirwin, P., Beller, S., Wolkowitz, W., & Pickar, D. (1988). Early parental loss and development of adult psychopathology. <u>Archives of General Psychiatry, 45,</u> 987-993.

Bozarth, A. R. (1986). <u>Life is Goodbye; Life is Hello: Grieving well through all kinds of loss.</u> Center City, MN: Hazelden Information and Educational Services.

Brennan, K. A. (1998). Attachment styles and personality disorders: Their connections to each other and to parental divorce, parental death, and perceptions of parental caregiving. <u>Journal of Personality, 66</u> (5), 835-878.

Brown, G. W., Harris, T. O., & Bifulco, A. (1986). Long-term effects of early loss of parent. In M. Rutter, C. E. Izard, & P. Read (Eds.), <u>Depression in young people: Developmental and clinical perspectives</u> (pp. 251-297). New York, NY: Guilford Press.

Chethik, N. (2001). <u>Fatherloss: How sons of all ages come to terms with the deaths of their dads.</u> New York, NY: Hyperion.

Christ, G. H., Siegel, K., & Sperber, D. (1994). Impact of parental terminal cancer on adolescents. <u>American Journal of Orthopsychiatry, 64</u> (4), 604-612.
Christ, G. H. (2000). <u>Healing children's grief: Surviving a parent's death from cancer.</u> New York, NY: Oxford University Press.

Davidman, L. (2000). <u>Motherloss.</u> Los Angeles, CA: University of California Press.

Dietrich, D. R., & Shabad, P.C. (1989). <u>The problem of loss and mourning.</u> Madison, CT: International Universities Press.

Dilworth, J. L., & Hildreth, G. J. (1997). <u>OMEGA, 36</u> (2), 147-159.
Dowdney, L., Wilson, R., Maughan, B., Allerton, M., Schofield, P., & Skuse, D. (1999). Psychological disturbance and service provision in parentally bereaved children: Prospective case-control study. <u>BMJ, 319,</u> 354-357.

Edelman, H. (1994). Motherless daughters. New York, NY: Delta Publishing.

Elizur, E., & Kaffman, M. (1983). Factors influencing the severity of childhood bereavement reactions. American Journal of Orthopsychiatry, 53, 668-676.

Emswiler, M. A., & Emswiler, J. P. (2000). Guiding your child through grief. New York, NY: Bantam Books.

Finkelstein, H. (1988). The long-term effects of early parent death: A review. Journal of Clinical Psychology, 44 (1), 3-9.

Floyd, G. (1999). A grief unveiled: One father's journey through the death of a child. Brewster, MA: Paraclete Press.

Fristad, M. A., Jedel, R., Weller, R. A., & Weller, E. B. (1993). Psychosocial functioning in children after the death of a parent. American Journal of Psychiatry, 150, 511-513.

Furman, E. (1974). A child's parent dies: Studies in childhood bereavement. New Haven, CT: Yale University Press.
Furman, E. (1983). Studies in childhood bereavement. Canadian Journal of Psychiatry, 28 (4), 241-247.

Furman, E. (1984). Children's patterns in mourning the death of a loved one. In H. Wass & C. Corr (Eds.), Childhood and death (pp. 185-203). Washington, DC: Hemisphere Publishing.

Gay, M. J., & Tonge, W. L. (1967). The late effects of loss of parents in childhood. British Journal of Psychiatry, 113, 753-759.

Harrington, R., & Harrison, L. (1999). Unproven assumptions about the impact of bereavement on children. Journal of the Royal Society of Medicine, 92, 230-233.
Harris, M. (1995). The loss that is forever: The lifelong impact of the early death of a mother or father. New York, NY: Penguin Books.

Heinzer, M. M. (1995). Loss of a parent in childhood: Attachment and coping in a model of adolescent resilience. Holistic Nursing Practice, 9, (3), 27-37.

James, J. W. & Friedman, R. (1998). The grief recovery handbook: The action program for moving beyond death, divorce, and other losses. New York, NY: Harper Perrenial.

Johnson, L. D. (1995). The mourning after death. Macon, GA: Smyth & Helwys Publishing, Inc.

Knight, K. H., Elfenbein, M. H., & Capozzi, L. (1998). Relationship of recollections of first death experience to current death attitudes. Death Studies, 24, 201-221.

Kopp, H. H. (1998). Daddy, where were you?: Healing for the father-deprived daughter. Ann Arbor, MI: Servant Publications.

Krementz, J. (1981). How it feels when a parent dies. New York, NY: Alfred A. Knopf, Inc.

Kubler-Ross, E. (1986). Death: The final stage of growth. New York, NY: Touchstone.

Kubler-Ross, E. (1997). On death and dying. New York, NY: Touchstone.

Kubler-Ross, E. (1997). Questions and answers on death and dying. New York, NY: Touchstone.

Kuening, D. A. (1987). Helping people through grief. Minneapolis, MN: Bethany House Publishers.
Kuntz, B. (1991). Exploring the grief of adolescents after the death of a parent. Journal of Child Adolescent Psychiatric Mental Health Nursing, 4 (3), 105-109.

Lewis, C. S. (1961). A grief observed. San Francisco, CA: Harper

San Francisco.

Lindemann, E. (1944). Symptomatology and management of acute grief. American Journal of Psychiatry, 101, 141-148.

Linn, M., Linn, D., & Fabricant, S. (1985). Healing the greatest hurt. Mahwah, NJ: Paulist Press.

Lohnes, M. A., & Kalter, N. (1994). Preventive intervention groups for parentally bereaved children. American Journal of Orthopsychiatry, 64 (4), 594-603.

Leucken, L. J. (1998). Attachment and loss experiences during childhood are associated with adult hostility, depression, and social support. Journal of Psychosomatic Research, 49, 85-91.

Luecken, L. J. (1998). Childhood attachment and loss experiences affect adult cardiovascular and cortisol function. Psychosomatic Medicine, 60, 765-772.

Mahon, M. M. (1999). Secondary losses in bereaved children when both parents have died: A case study. OMEGA, 39 (4), 297-314.

Maier, E. H., & Lachman, M. E. (2000). Consequences of early parental loss and separation for health and well-being in midlife. international Journal of Behavioral Development, 24 (2), 183-189.

Marshall, F. (1993). Losing a parent. Tucson, AZ: Fisher Books.

Martin, J. D., & Ferris, F. D. (1992). I can't stop crying: It's so hard when someone you love dies. Toronto, Ontario: Key Porter Books Limited.
Marwit, S. J., & Carusa, S. S. (1998). Communicated support following loss: Examining the experiences of parental death and parental divorce in adolescence. Death Studies, 22, 237-255.

McLouglin, J. (Ed.). (1994). On the death of a parent. London,

England: Virago Press.

Mitsch, R., & Brookside, L. (1993). <u>Grieving the loss of someone you love: Daily meditations to help you through the grieving process.</u> Ann Arbor, MI: Servant Publications.

Mulcahey, A. L., & Young, M. A. (1995). A bereavement support group for children: Fostering communication about grief and healing. <u>Cancer Practice, 3</u> (3), 150-156.

Nuttall, D. (1997). The needs of bereaved people at the time of the funeral. In P. C. Jupp & T. Rogers (Eds.). <u>Interpreting death: Christian theology and pastoral practice.</u> Herndon, VA: Cassell.

Osterweis, M., Solomon, F., & Green, M. (Eds.). (1984). <u>Bereavement: Reactions, consequences and care.</u> Washington, DC: national Academy Press.

Rando, T. (1988). <u>How to go on living when someone you love dies.</u> New York, NY: Bantam Books.

Raveis, V. H. (1999). Children's psychological distress following the death of a parent. <u>Journal of Youth and Adolescence, 28</u> (2), 165-180.

Richter, J., Eisemann, M., Richter, G., & Perris, C. (1992). Determinants of recall of parental rearing behavior. <u>Psychopathology, 25,</u> 120-127.

Rosenblatt, P., & Elde, C. (1990). Shared reminiscence about a deceased parent: Implications for grief education and grief counseling. <u>Family Relations, 39,</u> 206-210.

Rosenheim, E., & Reicher, R. (1986). Children in anticipatory grief: The lonely predicament. <u>Journal of Clinical Child Psychology, 15</u> (2), 115-119.

Saldinger, A., Cain, A., Kalter, N., & Lohnes, K. (1999). Anticipating parental death in families with young children.

American Journal of Orthopsychiatry, 69 (1), 39-48.

Siegel, K., Karus, D., & Raveis, V. H. (1996). Adjustment of children facing the death of a parent due to cancer. Journal of the American Academy of Child Adolescent Psychiatry, 35 (4), 442-450.

Simon, L., & Drantell, J. J. (1998). A music a no longer heard. New York, NY: Simon & Schuster.

Silverman, P. R., Nickman, S., & Worden, J. W. (1992). Detachment revisited: The child's reconstruction of a dead parent. American Journal of Orthopsychiatry, 62 (4), 494-503.

Silverman, P., & Worden, W. (1992). Children's reactions in the early months after the death of a parent. American Journal of Orthopsychiatry, 62, 93-104.

Smith, H. I. (1994). On grieving the death of a father. Minneapolis, MN: Augsburg Fortress.
Smith, H. I. (1995). Death and grief: Healing through group support. Minneapolis, MN: Augsburg Fortress.

Smith, S. C., & Pennels, M. (Eds.). (1995). Interventions with bereaved children. London, England: Jessica Kingsley Publishers.

Staudacher, C. (1991). Men & grief. Oakland, CA: New Harbinger Publications.

Strommen, M. P., & Strommen, A. I. (1996). Five cries of grief: One family's journey to healing after the tragic death of a son. Minneapolis, MN: Augsburg Fortress.
Taylor, R. (1992). When life is changed forever: By the death of someone near. Eugene, OR: Harvest House Publishers.
Teakle, H. (1992). My daddy died: Supporting young children in grief. North Blackburn Victoria, Australia: Collins Dove.

Tengbom, M. (1989). Grief for a season. Minneapolis, MN:

Bethany House Publishers.

Thompson, M. P., Kaslow, N. J., Kingree, J. B., King, M., Bryant, L., & Rey, M. (1998). Psychological symptomatology following parental death in a predominantly minority sample of children and adolescents. Journal of Clinical Child Psychology, 27 (4), 434-441.
Thompson, M. P., Kaslow, N. J., Price, A. W., Williams, K., & Kingree, J. B. (1998). Journal of Abnormal Child Psychology, 26 (5), 357-366.

Tremblay, G. C., & Israel, A. C. (1998). Children's adjustment to parental death. Clinical Psychology: Science and Practice, 5, 424-438.

Van Eerdewegh, M., Bieri, M. D., Prilla, R. H., & Clayton, P. J. (1982). The bereaved child. British Journal of Psychiatry, 140, 23-29.

Wessel, M. A. (1996). When children mourn a loved one. In H. M. Spiro, M. G. McCrea Curnen, & L. P. Wandel (Eds.), Facing death. New Haven, CT: Yale University Press.

Wolpe, D. (1999). Making loss matter: Creating meaning in difficult times. New York, NY: Riverhead Books.

Worden, J. W., & Silverman, P. R. (1996). Parental death and the adjustment of school-age children. Omega, 33, (2), 91-102.

Wright, H. N. (1993). Recovering from the losses of life. Grand Rapids, MI: Fleming H. Revell.

Zambelli, G. C., Clark, E. J., Barile, L., & de Jong, A. F. (1988). An interdisciplinary approach to clinical intervention for childhood bereavement. Death Studies, 12, 41-50.

Printed in the United States
828200004B

9 781591 603450